The Physiology of Emotional and Irrational Investing

The financial markets are a rollercoaster, and this book follows the same theme: the seduction of money; our ruinous, heady and high stakes pursuit of it; the incredible fortunes and calamitous losses that have been made in its name; the new and significant threat of retail (armchair) investors wanting their piece of the pie; and the perpetual and foolish mismatch that has always existed and will always exist between our evolutionary programming and the design of the financial markets.

The dominant theme that runs throughout the book ('Working out Wall Street') is actually a play on words, and relates to the need both to *work out* why Wall Street traders act so irrationally (e.g. using behavioural finance and evolutionary design to explain herding and panic selling) and to use physiological and sport science-related approaches to explain why *working out* (i.e. adopting exercise and diet-related practices usually applied to athletes) can significantly counter these behaviours. The phrase 'animal spirits' utilised in the concluding chapter title ('Taming animal spirits') refers to the seminal work of John Maynard Keynes in his 1936 classic work, *The General Theory of Employment, Interest and Money*, and the idea that human emotions – animal spirits – remain a significant driver in (irrational and emotional) investing.

The rationale for this book is clear; behavioural finance and neurofinance have opened the floodgates in terms of recognising the role of emotional investing in cyclical boom-and-bust scenarios, but what is still missing is an answer to the question *So what do we do about it?* This book seeks, in as compelling and entertaining a fashion as possible, to provide that answer.

Elesa Zehndorfer is Research Associate at Manchester Metropolitan University, UK, Research Officer for British Mensa and Quora Top Writer 2017.

The Physiology of Emotional and Irrational Investing

Causes and Solutions

Elesa Zehndorfer

Routledge
Taylor & Francis Group

LONDON AND NEW YORK

First published 2018
by Routledge
2 Park Square, Milton Park, Abingdon, Oxon OX14 4RN

and by Routledge
711 Third Avenue, New York, NY 10017

Routledge is an imprint of the Taylor & Francis Group, an informa business

British Library Cataloguing-in-Publication Data
A catalogue record for this book is available from the British Library

Library of Congress Cataloging-in-Publication Data
Names: Zehndorfer, Elesa, author.
Title: The physiology of emotional & irrational investing : causes and solutions / Elesa Zehndorfer.
Other titles: Physiology of emotional and irrational investing
Description: Abingdon, Oxon ; New York, NY : Routledge, 2018. | Includes bibliographical references and index.
Identifiers: LCCN 2017039733 (print) | LCCN 2017047218 (ebook) | ISBN 9781315269368 (eBook) | ISBN 9781138284630 (hardback : alk. paper)
Subjects: LCSH: Investments—Psychological aspects. | Speculation—Psychological aspects. | Speculation—Physiological aspects.
Classification: LCC HG4515.15 (ebook) | LCC HG4515.15 .Z44 2018 (print) | DDC 332.601/9—dc23
LC record available at https://lccn.loc.gov/2017039733

ISBN: 978-1-138-28463-0 (hbk)
ISBN: 978-1-315-26936-8 (ebk)

Typeset in Times New Roman
by Apex CoVantage, LLC

**For
Henry and Clemens**

Contents

Figures

Acknowledgements

Many experts have contributed their time and expertise to this book, for which I am extremely grateful. I reserve particular thanks for Jeffrey Klink, CEO of Klink & Co. Inc.; Dermot Murphy, Managing Director and Head of Global Loans and Special Situations Group at HSBC; Jack Rees, associate news producer; Heidi Hanna, leading stress expert; Dr Natalie Darko, leading sports sociologist; and Jon Harris, World Champion bodybuilder and coach. Great thanks also to the senior, and greatly knowledgeable, financial markets experts whose roles required their anonymisation within the pages of this book. Their combined words made the theory contained in this book really come alive.

I also owe a real debt of gratitude to my editor, Kristina Abbotts, who championed this book from the outset. Without your belief in the project, I might never have had the chance to write this book.

Finally, I cannot thank my friends and family enough for your help and support. Great thanks are due in particular to my husband Clemens for all of his supportive comments and motivation. Lastly, and most importantly, I reserve my greatest thanks for my little boy, Henry. I know that you will read this book one day, Henry, and I want you to know that everything I write is inspired by, and for, you.

1 Introduction

Banks should train traders like athletes.

— Professor John Coates (2012b)

Working out Wall Street: taming animal spirits

The financial markets are a rollercoaster,[1] and this book follows the same theme – the seduction of money; our ruinous, heady and high stakes pursuit of it; the incredible fortunes and calamitous losses that have been made in its name; and the perpetual and foolish mismatch that has always existed – and will always exist – between our evolutionary programming and the design of the financial markets. Whilst behavioural finance and neurofinance have opened the floodgates in terms of recognising the role of neurological and physiological factors in emotional, irrational investing, what is still missing is an answer to the question *So what do we do about it?* This book seeks – in as compelling and entertaining a fashion as possible – to provide that answer.

Sports science encapsulates four distinct sciences: physiology, psychology, motor control/learning and biomechanics. Physiology, in particular, offers incredible insights into maximising human performance in banks and on trading desks, just as it offers incredible insights into athletic performance. This is because the role of neurotransmitters such as dopamine and serotonin, and endogenous steroids such as cortisol and testosterone, provide utterly compelling insights into human performance – not only on the sports field but also in financial markets. It is a concept that forms a fundamental foundation of this book.

Sport physiology poses a fundamental question: 'the role genetics plays in the attainment of world class status and truly elite athletic performance' (Joyner & Coyle, 2007, p. 35) – not only in absolute terms but in the context of 'asking fundamental questions about the ability of various animal species to function in harsh environments' (ibid.). Evaluating the interaction of the trader's physiology with the harsh environment in which he works (the financial markets) offers fascinating insights into human behaviour that can lead to the optimisation of his trading and investing behaviours, just as sports physiology leads to optimisation of athletic performance.

The two-part structure of this book is a play on words, relating to the need to 'work out' why Wall Street and Main Street traders act, at times, so irrationally (e.g. herding, panic selling), and to explain how 'working out' (i.e. adoption of exercise and diet-related practices utilised by athletes and coaches) can significantly counter these behaviours.[2] The phrase 'animal spirits' refers to the seminal work of John Maynard, *The General Theory of Employment, Interest and Money* (1936), and the idea that human emotions remain a significant driver in (irrational and emotional) investing.[3] As stated by Coates (2014), 'we can see that the risk-taking pathologies found in traders also lead chief executives, trial lawyers, oil executives and others to swing from excessive and ill-conceived risks to petrified risk aversion' and that a knowledge of the physiological factors that underlie irrational and emotional decision-making will allow us to 'manage these risk takers, much as sport physiologists manage athletes, to stabilise their risk taking and lower stress. And that possibility opens up exciting vistas of human performance' (Coates, 2014). It is this very opportunity – to open up vistas of human performance via the use of sport science principles – that this book seeks to address.

Working out Wall Street: structure of the book

Part I of the book ('Working out Wall Street' – Chapters 1–3) focuses, subsequently, on drilling down into the physiology of the trader and investor to understand how physiological design and sociological factors collude to force irrational, emotional investing to occur. A key historical omission of emotions in financial markets analysis is tracked to an attempted unification of sciences in the 1930s, with observations made as to how this omission has led to fundamental weaknesses in predicting boom-and-bust scenarios. An entertaining recollection of the central role of hedonism in earlier economic theory – which sits well with the hedonistic world of trading as we understand it today – is considered here as well. Psychology also plays a key role in the book in understanding how the mind of a great trader needs to be nurtured to avoid incredible downsides (e.g. fraud, insider trading, herding, gambling addictions) – just as any great coach needs to understand how the incredible focus, goal orientation and ambition of a talented athlete needs significant attention. Great performance never just happens.

Part II of the book ('Taming animal spirits' – Chapter 4) focuses on the 'what do we do about it' question, to work out how to tame animal spirits using principles of exercise physiology (e.g. cardiovascular and strength training, meditative techniques and relaxation strategies, diet and supplementation, restorative recreation via exposure to nature).

The book combines scientific theoretical insight with the entertaining and thought-provoking words of financial experts in a series of exclusive 'Special features'. This allows the book to deliver an unusually applied, pragmatic body of knowledge to all readers. It is hoped that the reader subsequently feels empowered both professionally and personally by the knowledge gained from the insights included in these pages.

Chapter 2

Money: a love story

> If we are to survive, we need to pursue rewards and avoid risks as quickly as possible.
>
> — Jason Zweig (2007, p. 14)

The effect exerted on our brain by thinking about, and trading, money is so strong that it actually mimics the effects of falling in love or taking cocaine or heroin (Lea & Webley, 2006).[4] This means that when a trader switches on his Bloomberg terminal at the start of a trading day and sees the monetary value of investments tracking across the screen, the limbic region of the brain simultaneously innervates his reward centre, producing a pleasurable sensation: the investing process becomes emotionally motivated from the outset. Little wonder, then, that parallels have been drawn by many authors between gambling and trading, given that they both offer seemingly limitless opportunities to activate the brain's reward and pleasure centre. Also, risk can itself be characterised as a feeling (Baddeley, 2013, p. 160), suggesting that a trader's very vocation is governed by emotion.

Common facets of irrational investing, such as euphoria and fear (in other words, shifts in risk preferences), are attributable to elevated levels of steroid hormones such as corticosteroids and testosterone (Coates et al., 2010), which strongly affect our ability to act rationally and cope with stress (De Kloet, 2000); 'economic agents are more hormonal than is assumed by theories of rational expectations' (Coates et al., 2010, p. 339). It is unsurprising in this context that assumptions of rationality in economics have been extensively questioned, with Elster (1996) commenting that 'economists have totally neglected the most important aspect of their subject matter' (p. 1386).

Whilst rational expectations theory asserts that individuals do not make systemic mistakes and that individuals use all available information efficiently (Baddeley, 2010, p. 281), it is an assumption critiqued widely by many post-classical economics and behavioural finance theorists (e.g. Keynes, 1937; Minsky, 1975; Kindleberger & Aliber, 2005). Certainly, it is a critique also implicitly supported by many other disciplines. The secretion of glucocorticoids in the face of stress (e.g. during a violent market swing), for example, exerts widespread effects on emotion and cognition (De Kloet, 2000) and can influence negatively the parts of the brain (e.g. hippocampus) responsible for economic decision-making (Coates et al., 2010). Testosterone secretion (which peaks during successful trading activity but can cause subsequent trading decisions to be overly risky) can be addictive (Kashkin & Kleber, 1989), whilst long-term exposure to stressful environments (such as trading in a bearish market) can blunt the brain's response to dopamine and cortisol and lead to an inability to cope with stress.

In order to find out more about this concept, the reader is introduced to irrational, emotional investing behaviours and to the role of neurological factors in predisposing us to their emergence – e.g. the 'house money effect' (why gamblers are more likely to continue to gamble if they are winning; see Barberis & Thaler, 2003, p. 1084) and *androgenic priming* (how testosterone rises in the face of a challenge, and after a victory; see Coates & Herbert, 2008, p. 6170). Anabolic steroids are addictive (Kashkin & Kleber, 1989), suggesting that traders experiencing androgenic priming may regularly seek out riskier trades to satiate cravings. Further, whilst short term effects of raised testosterone can be positive, longer term elevation 'promotes confidence and fearlessness in the face of novelty' (Coates et al., 2010, p. 337), which can lead to more aggressive and overly optimistic trading.[5]

Evolutionary biology, for example, tells us that the phenomenon of *herding* is not irrational in itself, as it occurs as a result of our evolutionary programming – in other words, it represents a survival instinct (Baddeley, 2010).[6] But placed in a trading scenario, it can clearly lead to negative consequences.

A running theme entitled 'Nature vs. the markets' (see Figure 1.8, and also Chapter 4) offers a compelling look at the ways in which our own evolutionary design, and the design of the financial markets, represent a fundamental mismatch that facilitates emotional and irrational decision-making. For example, we are hardwired to react emotionally – not rationally – when faced with a pressured or stressful environment. In the markets, this can easily lead to an unprofitable knee-jerk decision through fear of losing out on profits, but in Palaeolithic times, emotionally reacting, through fear, to a dangerous animal and running to safety would have saved us. Evolutionary behaviour of this type is exacerbated by the seductive effect of money (as noted on p. 120), a tendency toward hubris and charismatic rhetoric in market commentary ('financial porn'; see Chapter 3) and the fast-paced and volatile nature of the financial markets, all of which combine to exert a powerful disruptive effect on one's ability to remain rational (Elster, 1996; Camerer et al., 2005; Gutnik et al., 2006).

Chapter 3

Trading long or short on stress?

> Out of all of the sections of finance, no position do I know of that is more extreme in terms of the emotional endurance one has to have than investment banking.
>
> — Psychologist Alden Cass (in Wieczner, 2014)

Traders 'live or die by their P&L' (quoted in Zehndorfer, 2015, p. 44), meaning that the inability to perform as well as one's peers can lead to potential dismissal – whereas the ability to generate P&L successfully can lead to large bonuses. The trading environment is extremely stressful and the volatility that characterises the markets exacerbates a dangerous likelihood for chronic over-production of cortisol in traders (Coates & Herbert, 2008). Given that cortisol has been found to be particularly sensitive to 'situations of uncontrollability, novelty and uncertainty' (Coates et al., 2010, p. 337), it is logical to surmise that financial markets actors remain exceptionally susceptible to chronic cortisol over-production.

We know that cortisol is highly reactive to unpredictability, and that the financial markets are inherently unpredictable. This raises the spectre of chronic cortisol over-production in traders and investors. Consider the *fear index*, for example, formally known as the S&P 500 Volatility Index, or VIX (Figure 1.1 overleaf).

A trader or investor actively engaging in the markets during the height of the Global Financial Crisis (September 2008 to March 2009) would have been exposed to historic levels of volatility and – subsequently – a likely overexposure to cortisol. Over-production of cortisol increases the likelihood that one perceives risk where it does not exist (McEwen, 1998b) and leads to a generally impaired ability to moderate risk (Coates et al., 2010). Given that the ability to manage risk constitutes the core function of a trader's role, cortisol over-production thus constitutes a significant danger within a financial markets environment. It also heightens perceptions of fear (Corodimas et al., 1994), leading to a tendency to lose faith in one's abilities (Kademian et al., 2005) – both clearly dangerous behaviours for a trader or investor. As cortisol downregulates dopamine, it also causes anxiety and depression, weakens the immune system, impairs general cognition, enhances the pathology of a multitude of illnesses and medical conditions and increases the storing of abdominal fat. In summary, it is a danger that needs to be managed.

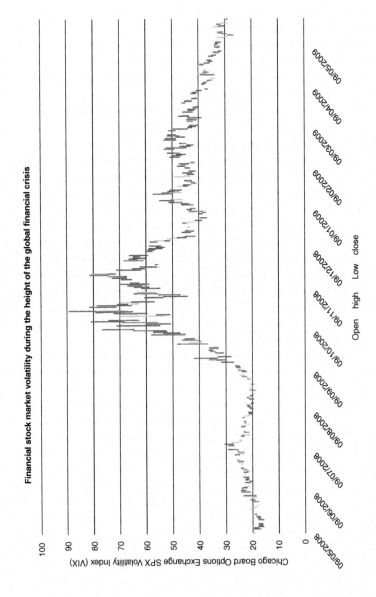

Figure 1.1 An unprecedented jump in the VIX

In the uncertain and highly stressful context of the financial markets, the pressures of trading are likely to significantly exacerbate stress-related physiological responses (e.g. the over-production of cortisol, the downregulation of dopamine and serotonin, adrenal fatigue):

> The people in trading often work incredibly long hours – 80 to 100 hours a week – and this is how you get ahead. People can maintain that for a few years, but then it starts to have a very serious effect on mental health . . . after five years of working like this, people suffer mental or physical breakdowns and one result of this is very poor judgement.
> (Spicer, cited in Winters, 2013, p. 24)

The rapid influx of 24/7 financial news, Twitter, and other social media news sources amplify this stress response, further exposing traders and investors to stressful variables and rendering them more vulnerable to cortisol over-production and irrational investing.

Indeed, studies have shown that traders' cortisol levels have been observed to rise as much as 500% in a day (Coates & Herbert, 2008, p. 6169) – a dangerous concept indeed when one considers that stress can cause brain shrinkage and an impaired ability to control impulses (Park, 2012). And it is a danger that can carry tragic consequences; the Center for Disease Control and Prevention (CDC) reports that 'sales representatives for financial and business services' (which includes investment advisers, brokers, traders and investment bankers) are 39% more likely to kill themselves than the workforce as a whole, with financial markets lawyers particularly at risk – lawyers are 54% more likely than the average worker to commit suicide (Wieczner, 2014). In an interview for *Fortune* (Wieczner, 2014), Wall Street psychologist Alden Cass commented that 'out of all the sections of finance, no position do I know of that's more extreme in terms of the emotional endurance one has to have than investment banking'. A recent spate of intern and student suicides, attributable in large part to an overwhelming pressure to succeed, raises the bar in terms of a need to get to the root cause of stress in finance. For example, 37% of a University of Notre Dame study of 1,200 finance professionals recently surveyed said that they had first-hand knowledge of unethical or illegal conduct in the workplace (University of Notre Dame & Labaton Sucharow LLP, 2015; see Chapter 3 for more details).

The chapter then considers the role of genetics and investing approaches to understand how contrarian investors (e.g. value investors, distressed debt investing, 'short sellers') are successful in trying to minimise market sentiment, herding and emotion, to instead rely on what legendary short seller Jim Chanos[7] refers to as financial detective work – a 'back to basics' approach that has, over the last 20 years, produced hedge fund returns 1.4 times higher than the wider equity market (e.g. the US S&P 500) with only half the volatility, and with distressed hedge funds logging an even more impressive 2.2 times higher returns (Zehndorfer, 2014, p. 49). Genetic variants that can cause some people to be more susceptible to stress than others (e.g. via presence of the L-MAOA gene, or L or S serotonin allele) are also discussed, as is the ever-prevalent threat of addictions, a danger that is heightened amongst traders and investors.

Chapter 4

Taming animal spirits

> Markets can remain irrational a lot longer than you and I can stay solvent.
> — John Maynard Keynes (quoted in Lowenstein, 2000, p. 123)

As stated by Coates (2014),

> if we view humans as embodied brains instead of disembodied minds, we can see that the risk-taking pathologies found in traders also lead chief executives, trial lawyers, oil executives and others to swing from excessive and ill-conceived risks to petrified risk aversion. It will also teach us to manage these risk takers, much as sport physiologists manage athletes, to stabilise their risk taking and lower stress. And that possibility opens up exciting vistas of human performance.

If the reader takes into account the extensive physiological and economic research presented throughout this book, it is of little surprise that Coates views the parallels between athletes and executives to be so sanguine. Subsequently, the focus of Part II, 'Taming animal spirits', explains why 'working out' – via the use of exercise and dietary- and lifestyle-related interventions – is proposed to offer a powerful effect on lowering irrational and emotional investing behaviours and, in doing so, increase the potential to maximise financial performance. But first, the reader is immersed in an account of just how responsive one's physiology is to one's environment. Nature is, as it turns out, way more powerful than we think in influencing our trading behaviours. Almost unbelievably, for example, scientific data identifies the impact of lunar cycles, geomagnetic storms, the weather and circannual variations in hormone levels in impacting cyclical trading and investing performance. It is an amazing observation, as powerful as data that builds an extremely strong and persuasive case for the utilisation of exercise in maximising trading and investing performance.

One of the most amazing outcomes of exercise, for example, is that it can completely reverse brain shrinkage caused by overexposure to cortisol/ stress and enable neurogenesis (the creation of new neurons in the brain) via the creation of BDNF (brain derived neurotrophic factors) proteins. It also increases DHEA (dehydroepiandrosterone, an adrenal steroid hormone), which acts as a protector to the over-production of cortisol, and norepinephrine, which helps the brain deal with stress more efficiently. Even one bout of exercise can lower aggression, with longer term engagement increasing serotonin (which plays a crucial role in innervating the whole brain, including cognitive function). Exercise gives the body 'a chance to practice dealing with stress. . . . This workout of the body's communication system may be the true value of exercise' (Dishman & Sothmann, 2005), with strength, cardiovascular and stretching-based exercise regimens offering significant, and striking, benefits.

Dietary interventions are extensive and include, for example, the fact that an insufficient carbohydrate (and overall calorific) intake exacerbates cortisol production, whilst ingestion of magnesium, B5 and Omega-3 supplements are positively correlated with lower cortisol and adrenaline secretion (e.g. Bauer et al., 2014, Sartori et al., 2012). Magnesium also increases sleep quality, which may exert a positive effect on stressed-out out executives who work long hours and who subsequently experience intermittent sleep deprivation (disrupted sleep can raise blood cortisol levels by as much as 45%; see e.g. Leproult et al., 1997).

Brief introductions

Before turning to the pages of the next chapter, however, it is first necessary to offer the reader some brief introductory information with regard to the basics of trading, the regions of the brain most affected by trading and the emotions associated with trading and investing. The book is, after all, a highly multidisciplinary one, so it is hoped that such an introduction will allow the reader to traverse the many concepts with far greater ease and enjoyment.

A brief guide to trading

Different kinds of trading and investing expose individuals to different physiological stressors. It is therefore useful at this juncture to provide the reader with a brief introduction to different kinds of trading (see Figure 1.2).

As the reader will note from the time continuum in Figure 1.2, an investor can hold investments for days, months or even years, whereas a trader can buy and sell within seconds. Investors hedge their investments by diversifying into a portfolio of stocks, and by adopting buy-and-hold strategies to ignore short-term fluctuations in profits and take a longer-term view. Traders, in comparison, operate with a much shorter-term focus, relying more heavily on momentum, market sentiment, short-term trends and price-data – whereas investors perform far more in-depth research. Retail traders, otherwise known as 'Main Street' traders, are generally less informed and usually engage with passive trading strategies and products (e.g. ETFs), whereas institutional or 'Wall Street' traders tend to be more informed and to utilise more mentally active trading and investing strategies. Traders generally greatly facilitate bubbles and busts and are heavily driven by market sentiment, whereas investors are often 'contrarian' in nature.

As the reader will note from Figure 1.2, the continuum of trading is quite complex, and the emotions evoked by each may subsequently be quite different. The reasons for these differences will, of course, become clearer throughout the pages of this book.

A brief guide to the brain

It would also help the reader, at this point, to engage in a very brief introduction to the brain and its effect on trading and investing. Throughout the pages of this book, you will hear a lot about **the prefrontal cortex** and **the limbic system** (Figure 1.3). The former is responsible for executive control, impulse control and rational decision-making. When orthodox economics theorists talk about assumptions of rationality of *homo economicus*, this area of the brain supports such a logic.

We are very rational when we engage our prefrontal cortex. However, we cannot be considered rational beings if we consider the dominance of the limbic region of the brain. The limbic system governs emotional reactions, pleasure and reward. It is in this area of the brain that all emotions – pleasure, fear, pain, excitement, joy – and the extreme behaviours that can result from them (addictions, herding, opportunistic greed, panic) – originate. As the reader will discover, money seduces us, giving greater power to our limbic system to react emotionally, not rationally, when we make trading decisions. It has been said that the emotional valence to large trades is diminished (Shariff et al., 2012, p. 131), meaning that we are emotionally weak when faced with the opportunity to acquire large amounts of money. So many aspects of the financial markets over-stimulate our limbic system; this is why emotional trading and investing, and the resulting boom-and-bust cycles so often seen in the financial markets, will never be extinguished. They can, however, be managed more efficiently; this is the focus of Chapter 4.

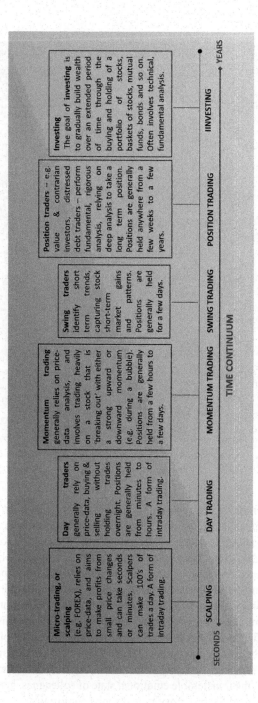

Micro-trading, or scalping
(e.g. FOREX), relies on price-data, and aims to make profits from small price changes and can take seconds or minutes. Scalpers can make 100's of trades a day. A form of intraday trading.

Day traders generally rely on price-data, buying & selling without holding trades overnight. Positions are generally held from minutes to hours. A form of intraday trading.

Momentum trading generally relies on price-data analysis, and involves trading heavily on a stock that is 'breaking out' with either a strong upward or downward momentum (e.g. during a bubble). Positions are generally held from a few hours to a few days.

Swing traders identify short term trends, capturing stock short-term market gains and patterns. Positions are generally held for a few days.

Position traders – e.g value & contrarian investors, distressed debt traders – perform fundamental, rigorous analysis, relying on deep analysis to take a long term position. Positions are generally held anywhere from a few weeks to a few years.

Investing
The goal of investing is to gradually build wealth over an extended period of time through the buying and holding of a portfolio of stocks, baskets of stocks, mutual funds, bonds and so on. Often involves technical, fundamental analysis.

SECONDS ← SCALPING · DAY TRADING · MOMENTUM TRADING · SWING TRADING · POSITION TRADING · INVESTING → YEARS

TIME CONTINUUM

Figure 1.2 An introduction to trading typologies

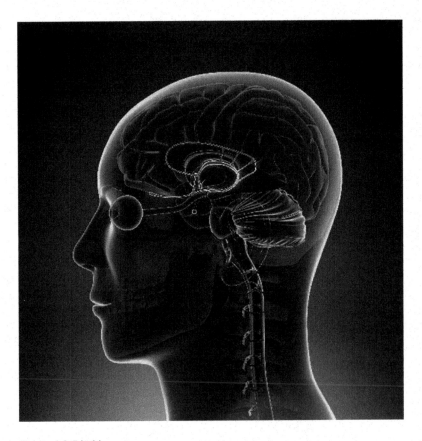

Figure 1.3 Limbic system

Both the prefrontal cortex and limbic regions of the brain exert a significant effect on financial preferences, decision-making and susceptibility to addictions and sensation-seeking behaviours (e.g. Tversky & Kahneman, 1974; Sapra & Zak, 2008; Kuhnen & Knutson, 2005). Conceptualising ourselves less as *homo economicus* and more as *homo biologicus* is potentially very empowering, as it opens the floodgates in recognising the value of exercise physiology and sport science in optimising a trader's physiology and, thus, performance. It also offers a great opportunity for this book to engage the reader in an introduction to a trader or investor's physiology and how it can be, and is, manipulated (both knowingly and unknowingly) by variables as seemingly eclectic as the media, lunar cycles, stock market unpredictability, the transferable emotional state of colleagues, genetics and an evolutionary need for rest, novelty and social conformity.

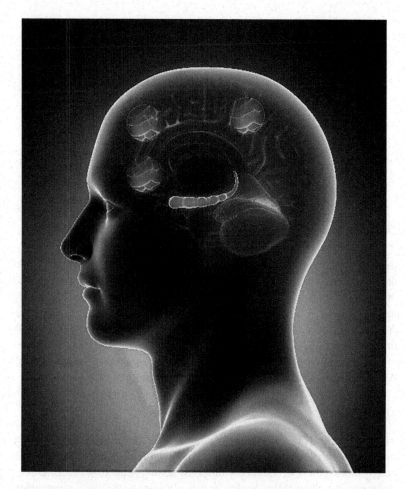

Figure 1.4 Prefrontal cortex and a portion of cortex occipital of the intra-parietal sulcus

A brief guide to investor emotions

Market sentiment and emotion are tremendous drivers of modern-day financial markets. A brief introduction to how they affect traders is, therefore, of great use to the reader.[8]

Figure 1.5 provides an effective visual representation of how traders and investors cycle through an initial period of indifference before being swept into a kind of emotional contagion including the often-observed investor behaviours of optimism, excitement and irrational exuberance. This can create a bubble (e.g. the 2005–2006 US housing boom), which can lead

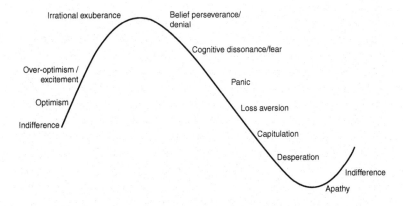

Figure 1.5 Cycle of trader and investor emotions

to an ensuing crash (e.g. the 2008 financial crisis – shown in Figure 1.5 as desperation and panic). This is usually characterised by a short-lived period of belief perseverance and denial before the bubble bursts (e.g. 2006–2007 investments in US housing debt, despite data indicating its toxicity). A period of capitulation and desperation then usually occurs (e.g. post-2008 financial crisis TARP – Troubled Asset Relief Program, and new banking regulations) before the entire cycle begins again (e.g. current Trump Administration efforts to repeal parts of the Dodd–Frank Act).

Homo biologicus

This book extends our understanding of the cycle illustrated in Figure 1.5 by pinpointing the physiology that cause emotional trading decisions to occur, and by linking these to commonly observed trading phenomena (e.g. *herding*, *churning* or *euphoria*) that lead to irrational trading and investing outcomes. For example, and with reference to Figure 1.5, our physiological instinct is to trade when we are most exuberant or euphoric (i.e. when stock prices peak and we are *least likely* to make a profit), and to become loss averse and unwilling to trade when experiencing desperation (i.e. when prices are lowest and we would be *most likely* to make a profit) (see Figure 1.6).

These concepts are explained in far greater depth throughout the book, but it is useful at this introductory stage to acknowledge the compelling role of *homo biologicus* (the reality of how man is biologically constructed) in shaping the trading and investing world – and to consider just how different he is to *homo economicus* (the theory of economic,

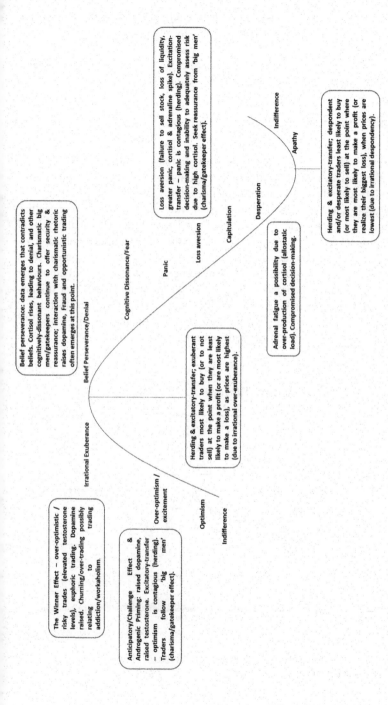

Figure 1.6 Understanding *homo biologicus*

The Winner Effect – over-optimistic / risky trades (elevated testosterone levels), euphoric trading. Dopamine raised. Churning/over-trading possibly relating to trading addiction/workaholism.

Anticipatory/Challenge Effect & Androgenic Priming: raised dopamine, raised testosterone. Excitatory-transfer – optimism is contagious (herding). Traders follow 'big men' (charisma/gatekeeper effect).

Herding & excitatory-transfer: exuberant traders most likely to buy (or to not sell) at the point when they are least likely to make a profit (or are most likely to make a loss), as prices are highest (due to irrational over-exuberance).

Belief perseverance: data emerges that contradicts beliefs, leading to denial, and other cognitively-dissonant behaviours. Cortisol rises. Charismatic big men/gatekeepers continue to offer security & reassurance; interaction with charismatic rhetoric raises dopamine. Fraud and opportunistic trading often emerges at this point.

Loss aversion (failure to sell stock, loss of liquidity, greater panic, cortisol & adrenaline spike). Excitation-transfer – panic is contagious (herding). Compromised decision-making and inability to adequately assess risk due to high cortisol. Seek reassurance from 'big men' (charisma/gatekeeper effect).

Adrenal fatigue a possibility due to over-production of cortisol (allostatic load). Compromised decision-making.

Herding & excitatory-transfer: despondent and/or desperate traders least likely to buy (or most likely to sell) at the point where they are most likely to make a profit (or realize their biggest loss), when prices are lowest (due to irrational despondency).

Indifference

Optimism

Over-optimism / excitement

Irrational Exuberance

Belief Perseverance/Denial

Cognitive Dissonance/Fear

Panic

Loss aversion

Capitulation

Desperation

Apathy

Indifference

rational man, which is socially constructed), which has been used, for decades, to shape economic thought. The former finds the natural environment to be a logical – some might say perfect – fit for his physiological responses, whereas a day trader experiences a constant schism of *nature vs. the markets.*

Predicting market sentiment

Are emotions a salient indicator of profit and losses? Indicators such as the MarketPsych Fear Index (Figure 1.7), Citigroup's Panic/Euphoria Model, and the Barclays Cycle of Investor Emotions certainly aim to capitalise on emotion-related data to gain a predictive edge.

Models such as these remain in relatively early stages of conceptual design, particularly relating to issues of predictive validity. What does nevertheless seem to be important is recognising the role of a trader's physiology in shaping his trading decisions (including the effect of physiological variables on emotions), as this would allow a deeper understanding of emotion-driven patterns of behaviour. It is also vital to acknowledge that trading does not take place in a vacuum, and to seek to understand the effect that a trader's environment (e.g. trading floor, during a financial crisis) exerts on his physiological and, subsequently, emotional reactions.

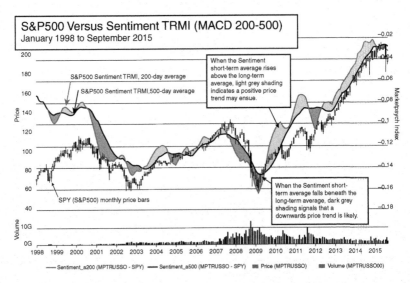

Figure 1.7 MarketPsych fear indicator 1998–2015. Permission granted by MarketPsych

Our genome has remained largely unchanged since Palaeolithic times. As hunter-gatherers, it made sense for our brain chemistry to favour emotion over rational logic to give us the necessary speed and force of action to ensure survival (e.g. a surge of testosterone and adrenaline when facing a wild animal would make us feel stronger and more courageous as well as more likely to fight, which would maximise survival). Figure 1.8 comprises two parts: a simplified overview of the biology of primitive man during a one-day cycle, and the biology of a modern-day trader during a one-day cycle.

When our Palaeolithic ancestor hunts, he experiences what behavioural finance experts would refer to as *androgenic priming*: when he sees an animal, his testosterone and adrenaline rise. Cortisol also rises in the short term, as does dopamine (the thrill of the chase). He physically moves in for the kill, requiring agility, strength and energy, and experiences the *winner effect* – a spike in testosterone and dopamine – after a successful kill. Enjoyment of the hunted wild animal with a social group meets requirements for the production of dopamine and oxytocin, a result of social bonding and pleasure, with cortisol returning to normal levels. The time taken to engage in the hunt and ingest food naturally leads to a period of rest, and a period of sleep during nocturnal hours before the cycle repeats itself the next day.

The day trader will also experience a rise in testosterone as he encounters *androgenic priming*, with the same short-term rise in testosterone, cortisol, adrenaline and dopamine. Following a successful trade, he experiences the *winner effect* and a surge in testosterone and dopamine similar to our Palaeolithic friend. Gratification, however, is far swifter; cortisol levels have no opportunity to return to healthy levels, as the trader does not enjoy a period of post-trade satiation, raising the risk of over-production of stress hormones (allostatic load will be addressed further later in this chapter) and adrenal fatigue. Testosterone and adrenaline remain raised, as there has been no utilisation of energy or strength in the 'action' phase. Dopamine levels may not rise particularly high if the day trader's dopaminergic response has been blunted from constant innervation due to a high volume of per diem trades. Dopamine may be increased, however, through the attainment of social status and prestige as a by-product of earning power.

Lunch is for wimps

Gordon Gekko, the eponymous anti-hero of Oliver Stone's movie classic *Wall Street* (1987), coined the memorable phrase 'lunch is for wimps', which 30 years later still provides an entertaining insight into the trader stereotype: leave the trading floor and you might miss out on a trade, so stay at your desk without taking a break. It is actually a great observation of a key mismatch

10,000-50,000BC: THE HUNTER-GATHERER IN HIS NATURAL ENVIRONMENT*

ANTICIPATE (hunting opportunity):

Testosterone, cortisol, adrenaline & dopamine are elevated (androgenic priming/anticipatory effect)

ACTION (execute hunt)

Testosterone, cortisol, dopamine raised

GRATIFICATION (makes successful kill)

Cortisol lowers as hunter enjoys a rest period after hunt to cook, eat and sleep. Oxytocin rises as he bonds with social group.

OUTCOME (eats well, seeks new hunting opportunity)

'The Winner Effect': Testosterone is raised which helps in future hunts. Dopamine rises in seeking/anticipating new hunt. Satiates hunger, well-rested.

RISKS: death or injury, hunger if not successful, lower social status if unsuccessful in hunt. Cortisol remains high if unsuccessful.

Figure 1.8a and b Nature *vs.* the markets

2017: THE DAY TRADER IN HIS NATURAL (FINANCIAL MARKETS) ENVIRONMENT*

ANTICIPATE (spot trading opportunity):

Testosterone, cortisol, adrenaline & dopamine are elevated (androgenic priming)

ACTION (place trade):

Testosterone, cortisol, dopamine raised

OUTCOME (makes profit, seeks new trade)

'The Winner Effect': Testosterone is raised which can lead to over-confidence in future trades. Cortisol remains raised due to market unpredictability, which can also cause compromised risk-taking. Dopamine rises in seeking/anticipating new trade

GRATIFICATION (makes successful trade).

Cortisol remains high due to market unpredictability, no rest period to allow cortisol to drop.

RISKS: lose money if not successful, lower social status if unsuccessful ('traders live & die by their P&L'), over-stimulation and lack of physical/cerebral rest leading to emotional and irrational responses

Figure 1.8a and b Nature *vs.* the markets

between the financial markets and our physiology that can be extrapolated onto Figure 1.8: timing. As indicated briefly on p. 17, our ancestors required and enjoyed rest between hunts. This naturally facilitated rest time into his natural cycle, as he would have taken a beast home to prepare and cook it. He would have shared it with family or a community, and allowed time to digest it. By the time the process was complete, it would be dark and impossible and/or dangerous to hunt, so he would have likely slept before beginning the process again the next day. Such a process respected his natural rhythm.

A day or swing trader, in comparison, has little to no opportunity to take a break. For a trader, breaks between trades can be almost non-existent, exposing the trader to the prospect of burnout, adrenal fatigue, artificially raised cortisol levels, stress addiction and irrationality (e.g. compromised decision-making) (see e.g. Bose et al., 2016). Given that the 'basic framework for physiologic gene regulation was selected during an era of obligatory physical activity, as the survival of our Late Paleolithic (50,000–10,000 BC) depended on hunting and gathering' (Booth et al., 2002, p. 399), we seem uniquely mismatched with an artificial environment of this kind. We still retain the animalistic instincts to hunt, gather and achieve basic survival of our Palaeolithic ancestors, but we do not allow ourselves the latitude of the rest and recovery time necessary to be able to repeat the process, ad infinitum, in a healthy and sustainable way.

It is interesting that the best coaches and athletes already recognise this differentiation between our ancestors' environments and those of modern man – e.g. periodisation or cycling of rest periods as a means of maximising optimal performance and minimising injuries and burnout (see e.g. Jones, 2002). Without these safeguards, cortisol, the body's stress hormone, can rise exponentially, stress addiction can occur and burnout and adrenal fatigue are very real threats (see Chapter 4). To cite former trader and professor John Coates:

> Risk managers could . . . learn from sport scientists how to spot and manage exuberance, fatigue and stress. They have to manage their traders much as coaches manage their athletes. And that means occasionally pulling them off the field until their biology resets.
>
> (Coates, 2012b)

This is, of course, a concept that forms a cornerstone of this book and is the foundation for Chapter 4.

Allostatic load

Another way we can compare the environment of our Palaeolithic ancestor with a modern-day trader is in the context of cortisol production. Our allostatic response (response to stress, including the secretion of cortisol) protects us in the short term but requires an adequate period of rest after which it can 'switch off' (see Figure 1.9).

Traders and investors are at risk of experiencing one of the four alternative scenarios in Figure 1.9 – i) over-stimulation of the allostatic response via repeated high volume trading, with very little built-in recovery time (e.g.

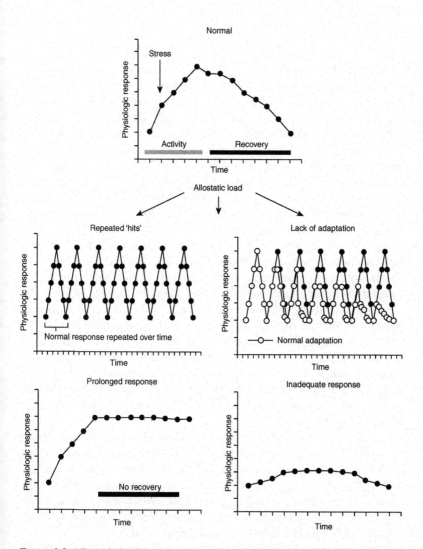

Figure 1.9 Allostatic load

Source: McEwen, B. S. (2000). Allostasis and allostatic load: Implications for neuropsychopharmacology. Elsevier Perspectives. *Neuropsychopharmacology*, 22, 2, 108–124 (p. 110).

constant day trading or swing trading); ii) a lack of adaptation caused by the 'wearing out' and over-stimulation of the stress response over time (e.g. a finance lawyer who faces a perpetually heavy workload with extremely long hours); iii) a delayed shutdown response (where the cortisol response malfunctions and cannot 'switch off'); and/or iv) an inadequate response caused by the 'wearing out' of stress pathways. Hippocrates was correct in stating, many centuries ago, that, 'rest, as soon as there is pain, is a great restorative in all disturbances of the body' (Aldrete & Aldrete, 2012, p. 210).

When we are talking about stress on a financial markets participant, what we are really referring to is the concept of 'allostatic load' (over-exposure to secretion of stress hormones), or 'allostasis' (the ability to achieve stability through change; see Sterling & Eyer, 1988). This is achieved via the use of a stress response system that utilises the autonomic nervous system, our HPA (hypothalamic–pituitary–adrenal) axis and our cardiovascular, immune and metabolic systems, which together respond to a stressful trigger. As noted by McEwen (1998), as we age, and particularly if we are consistently over-exposed to stress, this system suffers from wear and tear. Poor lifestyle choices, such as a sedentary lifestyle, alcohol and drug use, high fat and sugar consumption and so on, will make this wear and tear ultimately worse, wearing out the body's ability to 'shut off' the allostatic response and leading to chronic overexposure to stress hormones. Insulin resistance and greater abdominal bodyfat (also a major risk factor to Type II diabetes) have also been found to be positively correlated to allostatic load. So traders do not just display vulnerability from the rigours of their professional life – vulnerabilities remain amplified from poor lifestyles, too (see Figure 1.10)

Stress has a clearly definable biological basis, where uncertainty maximises the secretion of cortisol, our stress hormone. Given the habitual volatility and uncertainty that characterise the financial markets, it is of little surprise that cortisol spikes of up to 500% (Coates & Herbert, 2008) have been recorded in day traders. Cortisol levels are particularly sensitive to 'situations of uncontrollability, novelty and uncertainty' (Coates & Herbert, 2008, p. 6169), and are affected not by the rate of a trader's economic return but by the variance of return.

Pre-competition testosterone levels positively affect dominance over the competition only when cortisol levels are low (Mehta & Josephs, 2010), because cortisol downregulates androgen (testosterone) receptor levels (Tilbrook et al., 2000). Highly stressed traders and investors are therefore more likely to be paralysed by inaction (experience 'loss aversion') in a violent downswing as their testosterone levels – and, therefore, risk appetite – have been downregulated by excessive cortisol production.

Coates and Herbert (2008) concluded that 'the relationship between cortisol and volatility [is] strong enough to suggest there may be a biological

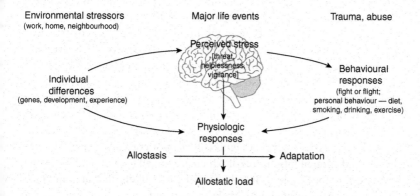

Figure 1.10 The stress response and development of allostatic load

Source: McEwen, B. S. (2000). Allostasis and allostatic load: Implications for neuropsychopharmacology. Elsevier Perspectives. *Neuropsychopharmacology*, 22, 2, 108–124 (p. 114).

substrate for the options market, a market of enormous size and influence in the global economy' (p. 6170), and also theorised that the over-activation of various regions of the brain could lead to investors exhibiting the irrational behaviours often observed in real markets (see Kuhnen & Knutson, 2005). In simpler terms: options traders might, as a result of the frequency of their trades and the high (cortisol-inducing) volatility of the options markets, experience a higher vulnerability than most to cortisol over-production and adrenal fatigue. They may, as we will discuss in Chapters 2 and 3, also be notably exposed to developing addictive and sensation-seeking trading behaviours.

For example, the volatility, uncertainty and sometimes fragility of the financial markets ultimately require a trader to remain consistently vigilant, which diminishes his ability to delay gratification (Shiv & Fodorikhin, 1999); the prefrontal cortex may become disconnected from other risk and reward areas of the brain in excessive risk takers, with the muting of intuitive signalling pathways a reason for excessive risk-taking in some traders (Sapra & Zak, 2010). Over the long-term, outcomes are precarious: 'elevated levels of testosterone could at some point begin to impair rational financial decision-making' (Coates et al., 2010, p. 339). To take one endogenous steroid as an example: testosterone is related to dominance under perceived situations of social status threat, with testosterone also a marker for aggression in the presence of high cortisol, further stressing the importance of managing both (Mehta & Josephs, 2010). When you factor in the use of stimulants (e.g. sugar, caffeine), depressants (e.g. alcohol) and lack of sleep (e.g. hosting client engagements as a regular requirement of one's role), these ill-effects can be exacerbated even further.

Crucially, uncertainty produces the highest increases in cortisol, even more so if a trader experiences a losing trade. This is absolutely critical to take into account for traders and investors, as the markets are constantly and unrelentingly unpredictable, often lurching between highs and lows and constantly throwing out the possibility of imminent crashes or opportunities. In other words, the unremitting power of the markets to constantly raise cortisol in traders, *regardless of whether they make a winning or losing trade*, places traders at significant risk of cortisol over-production, burnout and adrenal fatigue, all of which are linked to irrational (and long-term unprofitable) trading. In other words, it is likely that at some point their stress buffers will simply begin to wear out.

Trader physiology: key takeaways

Ultimately, physiology offers an incredibly additive insight into trader and investor irrationality. Key insights in this chapter include the following high-level facts;

- All emotional, irrational trading and investing behaviours observed in a boom-and-bust scenario (e.g. euphoria, panic, despondency) have clearly identifiable physiological antecedents. This book empowers traders and investors by educating them as to what these biological reactions are, and also extends our understanding of what behavioural finance reactions (e.g. herding) constitute on a purely physiological level;
- When we look at nature vs the markets, nature is the more powerful of the two; the financial markets indulge short-term impulses, which can lead to physiological reactions that compromise decision-making and our ability to take on risk. It is arguably impossible for us to trade rationally, because of the way we are evolutionarily designed to react to artificial situations such as those required – with frequency – of a trader or investor;
- Lack of rest between trades, including the stress of making contrarian trades (which goes against our natural instincts to follow the herd) remains a key driver in emotional trading – as it exacerbates the ongoing cortisol over-production to which traders are so frequently exposed;
- An evolutionary need to herd (follow the crowd) and to socially conform contributes notably to the euphoria phase in financial markets booms and the panic phase in financial markets busts;
- The typology of traders tells us that different types of traders (e.g. swing trader) will be exposed at differing levels to physiological reactions that make us irrational.

Special feature: money, seduction, profit and panic

'It's not your money, it's not your money, it's not your money'

I spoke with a successful Portfolio Manager at a multi-award-winning hedge fund with over $5 billion under management to understand the extreme emotions experienced in trading large amounts of money, and strategies that can be used to minimise emotional trading.

Q. How do you successfully manage your emotions, and how has this translated into more profitable outcomes?

Despite it sometimes being perceived as a glamorous career, being a professional investor can be a very humbling and levelling experience. No matter how smart, hardworking or accomplished you are, professionally and/or academically, the only thing that really matters at the end of the day in being successful is how volatile your returns are, how much risk you take to generate those returns, and how much absolute and sometime relative (e.g. relative to an index) P&L (profit) you generate.

A lot of extraneous factors are not under your control, which means that even very experienced investors can be wrong 30–40% of the time. That represents a very unusual set-up, if you compare that to most other professions, e.g. a lawyer or a medic.

What's also quite unique about the profession is that some investors can sometimes be more successful than you are just because they are lucky and you happen to be unlucky in the context of that particular trade. Arguably it is quite unusual that sometimes a random guy (remember the test of the monkey with the dartboard?) can be as – or even more – successful than a professional investor, which, again, is very difficult to image with other professions. Clearly over time, a certain edge of the professional investor (in name selection, trade construction, portfolio construction and/or risk management) should come through, but in the short-term one sometimes can look pretty stupid.

Consequently, it can sometime be very frustrating and emotionally draining to invest, even if you are a professional, as there always will be factors you cannot control, and that's really what is so emotionally draining – you are constantly operating in an uncertain environment.

One way to distance yourself from this is to try and be emotionally detached from the investment process, which sounds simple in theory, but in practice is almost impossible.

I remember when I was a young analyst on the trading desk, my head trader took me to the side during after work drinks. He was a very experienced investor and I had greatest respect for him. He must have realized that – as a young analyst – I was at times quite tense when positions would go against me, and he told me something I haven't forgotten to this day. He said, in all seriousness: 'When you are investing, always remember one thing: "it's not your money, it's not your money, it's not your money"'.

I was a bit perplexed at the time, and probably just laughed nervously but he was entirely serious. Only later in my career did I realise that this is indeed a quite healthy approach to stay more objective and focused on the task in hand (although in reality, in a hedge fund, usually meaningful amounts of monies of the investment professionals themselves are actually tied up in the fund, and therefore one clearly is (at least partially) trading with one's own money). Not to mention the career risk of course that if a trade goes materially against you there is always the very personal risk of being shown the door.

So while trying to detach yourself from the pecuniary aspect of investing is helpful, it is not enough. One also needs to have an action plan in place to proactively manage your emotions, to be prepared as and when they kick in (especially in volatile markets, when positions move against you (i.e. fear), or alternatively when you think (following a good run of good trades) that nothing can go wrong (i.e. greed). Disciplined profit-taking or stop-losses for example can make you less dependent on your emotions, as you are often just executing a pre-agreed plan as and when a certain situation arises. Also, a) probabilistic thinking (think in terms of a range of potential scenarios rather than one specific outcome that you consider to be certain), b) asymmetric trade construction (losing less money if you are wrong, than making money if you are right), and c) sensible portfolio construction (sufficient but not too much diversification and appropriate hedging) should allow you to remain emotionally more stable if different uncertain scenarios get realized.

Q. You go to the gym multiple times a week and eat very healthily. It is obviously positive for health-related reasons, but do you think that it benefits you professionally in any way?

The problem with professional investing sometimes can be that it is difficult to switch off. Especially these days with ubiquitous internet and email access it can be tempting to keep monitoring your investment portfolio constantly, especially if you are trading a global portfolio with US, European and Asian exposures which are active throughout different time zones during the day.

Like in any job though, it is important to get distance and perspective to the daily routine and working out is a very good way of doing this, as well as allowing you to get fitter at the same time – valuable in trading and investing which is mostly a desk-bound activity.

What I also found useful is that working out can divert your focus and attention in a good way. Especially if you sometimes had a tough day P&L-wise the previous day (which naturally can sometimes make you feel a bit useless), working out and achieving a certain fitness goal (x number of strokes on the rower, y number of rounds on the bike, z kg of weight lifted, etc.), can make you feel more accomplished and help re-set the clock so you are ready to take on the markets the following morning.

Since I started going to the gym, in the morning (especially after a couple of down-days), I find that the routine of working out can be quite cleansing. Prior to having taken up exercise, I would sometimes continue to be 'in a funk' the following day, which usually led to poor trading, like becoming nervous and overtrading, or becoming outright fearful and selling at the worst possible time.

Q. Thinking like a value investor/trader means being able to base decisions on logic, not emotion. How do you personally research, identify and execute a trade?

One of the most accomplished distressed and value investors for example repeatedly says: 'It's not what you buy it's what you pay for it', which essentially means that focusing on value (i.e. buying at a market price below the intrinsic value) is far more important than the asset that you actually buy. Many retail investors sometimes forget the importance of this. High quality investments can be very risky if you buy them at an inflated price while low quality investments can be beautiful investments if you buy them cheap enough.

It's really just the relationship between value and price that matters, and retail investors sometimes only focus on one side of the equation (e.g. 'buy Tesla') while ignoring the other (i.e. as to whether it is good value at this price).

Dealing with emotions can indeed be tricky, especially for less experienced investors, as our emotions can lead us to take very wrong actions. It is human nature for example to chase performance to buy what is giving us pleasure (gains) and to sell what is giving us pain (losses) – effectively buying high and selling low, but we clearly should do the opposite (buy low, sell high). While professional investors are clearly also exposed to this, they tend to have pre-determined trading strategies with active risk management strategies in place which can help to neutralize these emotional tendencies.

Q. *A huge stressor for you is how unpredictable the markets are becoming. Could you explain the root cause of this, and how it might contribute to bad trading decisions?*

Most markets at the time of writing this (June 2017) are indeed very dislocated. The business and credit cycle has been on an expansionary course since March 2009, in the midst of the financial crisis. Since then, over 8 years have passed, which is an unusually long period between crashes (the average is more like 5–6 years) and can and has been explained by the extraordinary amount of support and financial stimulus provided by the world's central banks. This wall of money provided by the central banks meant that a lot of investment strategies were successful, but one has to acknowledge that the cause for this performance was, in a lot of cases, less investor skill but more the extraordinary benign backdrop.

When I look at the cause of the next financial crisis, I'd say that it is difficult to pin-point the exact catalyst for a correction, but as always a) stretched valuations, b) very high expectations (of the current status quo continuing or indeed even improving from here due to Trump's expected tax cuts or infrastructure spending, etc.) and c) very long investor positioning. The latter, I feel, is particularly scary in relation to passive (including ETFs) and quantitative investment strategies which – according to JP Morgan's Global Head of Quantitative and Derivatives Strategy Marko Kolanovic – now account for 60% of all equity assets (versus less than 30% a decade ago). Retail investor trading in passive strategies, like ETFs, tend to also invest in assets or instruments that they don't really understand. At the same time the quantitative strategies can sometimes utilise very levered strategies like risk-parity strategies (which are currently increasing their exposures due to the low volatility environment – despite aggressive valuations). I'd say a combination of these factors provide, typically, a good starting point for a correction.

Combine this with d) an increasing leverage in the corporate space and a stretched and levered consumer (especially in the US), e) likely deteriorating earnings from here, and f) a likely volatility (political, geopolitical or otherwise) event (from very low current levels) which will add fuel to the fire – and we could be seeing a material correction in the next 6–12 months.

Q. *High-volume day trading can be highly stressful and fast-paced, whereas your speciality – distressed debt – is presumably a lot slower-paced. What are the most stressful aspects of being a trader in distressed debt?*

Clearly distressed trading is a contrarian investment strategy and as such can be inherently more stressful than investing in on-the-run performing situations.

Similar to a short seller who is expressing a negative view on a generally very well perceived company, a distressed investor is typically expressing a positive view on a generally very badly perceived company. As such you are naturally a minority and a majority will continuously and sometimes loudly tell you that you are wrong in your contrarian assessment.

As such this requires some mental stability and toughness. In addition to this, what also can be difficult is the sometimes very illiquid nature of distressed investing which is particularly difficult when investing in post-restructured equity positions. If a company for example has gone through a bankruptcy process during which all its debt was converted to equity, the company itself is usually in a very strong position balance-sheet wise (as there is typically no or little of financial debt post-emergence from bankruptcy). As such, the post-restructured equity position is fundamentally not that risky, but due to technical reasons (e.g. due to certain investors not being able to hold equity positions in their respective funds), they can sometimes trade very badly and sometimes can trade completely detached from underlying fundamentals.

This situation can become stressful for a distressed investor as the screen-price of the equity goes down, even though the value in most cases can be very compelling. At the same time, it is difficult to buy more given the low liquidity and, as such, one has to have patient capital to create an exit event (like a secondary offering, an IPO, a refinancing, M&A transaction or otherwise) which can take time – and patience.

Q. *Research indicates that traders tend to have high testosterone, which has the positive benefits of ability to take on risk, and a very strong focus, but a lot of negatives (e.g. association with fraud, aggression, overly risky trading, etc.). In the real world, does this hold any truth?*

I would say it depends. When I was working on trading desks at various investment banks it clearly was a sometimes testosterone-filled environment.

I remember an incident, for example, where a senior sales person got so angry with a trader that he smashed his phone and his computer screen and they screamed at each other for a while. Junior inexperienced traders can sometimes be quite obnoxious as they might think that 'being a dick' is part of their job description.

Everybody knows of a big-shot trader who ultimately blew himself up big time. These stories are surely sometimes a bit exaggerated, but in essence are just a function of how part of the system works. If you are successful, people give you more money, if you manage more money it a) becomes more difficult to invest this successfully and b) you might also get overconfident. Also, one has to bear in mind is that it is inherently difficult to continuously trade profitably so a culture of big profits and big losses is bound to emerge.

Q. Traders such as yourself risk cortisol over-production and adrenal failure, which is obviously negative for health and profit-generation. Are institutions aware of this risk?

Not to my knowledge. None of the three leading investment banks I worked for, or any hedge fund that I know, is aware of the physiological aspect of trading and investing. This area is in fact very much neglected. One tends to focus purely on the mental aspects which I feel is clearly a shortcoming. I heard some larger hedge funds might have experimented with this in some way, but I believe it is still in its infancy and therefore surely has a lot of potential.

I think that trader physiology is a useful concept for hedge funds and investment banks to acknowledge, in the context of how to improve performance, and a lot more should be done to understand and exploit it.

Special feature: the modern James Bond

I spoke to Frank Mason*, former infantry soldier and current Group Head of Crisis Management and IT Risk for an international stock *exchange. Frank discusses how the modern James Bond would now be an IT analyst, how tech enables market manipulation and how his British Army experiences shaped his ability to control emotions in a crisis.*

We are seeing a significant growth in malicious cyber activity in the open market and targeting financial institutions. In some cases, it is hacktivism – in others, it is common criminals. The cyber event in Bangladesh which netted $80million+ from their central bank recently, was perhaps the most successful cyber-attack to date . . . that we know of.

On cyber threats

Given events such as these, it is inevitable that these types of attacks will reoccur. The rewards are potentially enormous for the criminals, and with the right planning it is proving extremely difficult for governments to make arrests or prosecutions. I also believe that some rogue states do seek to implant staff into companies which have access to critical trade data or reporting systems. This is to enable real time access to information that no one else has – spying, 2017 style. James Bond now works as an IT analyst somewhere getting paid a lot more and is not being shot at. He is now also extremely hard to catch. Within the security world, this is known as the 'insider threat'. All agree this presents a very real and present danger.

Some will feel strongly that banking as an institution straddles the border of what is allowed, while the regulators play catch-up – in effect constantly pushing the boundaries in complex high value trade and deal structures which take years to understand. The movie *Too Big to Fail* provides a great example.

On fraud

In my experience, I'd suggest that the number and frequency of individual fraud is actually fairly low when compared to the number of people with access to trading systems and sensitive data. That said, when these folks do cross the line the numbers involved are mind boggling, and the impact that this has is significant – Bernie Madoff is a great example. Madoff destroyed the lives of many people through a huge fraud, which duped many of the world's largest financial institutions.

On the threat of market manipulation

Technology is impacting the way trading is performed, both positively and negatively. Traders today have more information available than ever before, and as such can make decisions of greater accuracy – conversely it could be argued that the prevalence of this much data is having an artificial effect on valuations. I do believe markets are sometimes artificially being manipulated, whether by design or by sheer volume of data being interpreted incorrectly is speculative.

I believe that with the recent prevalence of cyber-attacks, that a small well organised group can affect the market. They can do this in a number of ways. First, they can corrupt the data sets that the market uses with 'false news', thereby moving share value artificially. This in turn can see trading houses react in a way that is predictable, opening up the opportunity for the bad guys to trade against, knowing the direction a share value is about to head. This is complete market manipulation. I believe this is done today, and I believe it is very hard to detect quickly.

Any form of market manipulation is illegal – and I do agree that there are bad guys trying to force market opinion in one way or another.

I think it is also highly relevant to look at the availability of self-trading. Anyone can now trade on their phones, 24/7 – how they get their trading data is completely unknown, as such I'd suggest that these activities are confusing the traditional market indices. Banking traders look to the big market data players – Bloomberg, Reuters etc. . . . but I don't believe 'Mom and Pop' traders do. Instead, I suspect the majority of their decisions come from viral feeds on more socially intended platforms e.g. Facebook, or Twitter.

On the origins of future crises

I believe ultimately that financial crises will become more technically driven (cyber, social media sentiment etc.), rather than geopolitical or terrorism based.

On managing emotions

I served in an infantry fighting unit in Afghanistan before working in the financial markets. As such, I got to see people at the most extreme ends of the spectrum. I learnt to push myself in physical and psychological ways which I never knew I could. And these for me are now valuable life skills and experiences, which I use often.

Serving in the military does provide you with a perspective that is completely unique. Interestingly, banking as an industry attracts many ex-service personnel. This is because I believe these skills and experiences often set us apart from others – particularly during times of high stress.

One of the basic life skills a recruit is taught is resilience and self-reliance. This is because when deployed into combat you must work as an extremely well-oiled machine, where trust is paramount amongst comrades. To earn this trust, the military puts you through a training programme which equalises everyone, and where only the robust make it out. If you make it through the various courses and selection programmes, you immediately respect those who have also made it through.

When you leave the military and work in 'civvy street' (a civilian job), nothing they throw at you will ever be as tough or as demanding either physically or psychologically. As a result, high stress industries like banking find ex-military staff stoic and reliable. I find I can often identify an ex-service person simply by their reactions and behaviours, particularly those with an infantry background.

In terms of examples of where I've applied these various skills, I'd have to say I use them daily. But often I see it more clearly where I'm given projects or tasks which require a certain level of organisation of large groups of staff, or where I've been involved in incidents which have run for many hours at a high tempo. It is then that I draw upon those moments where I've been pushed beyond what I though was possible, and fairly easily pushed on through.

Working in the crisis management arena, we often are faced with events which require whole teams to work through the night, or through very long shifts for many days. This is where I tend to find my 'sweet spot' – that is to say, I find I am quite comfortable psychologically and never lose my grip on the perspective that 'no one is going to die because this application has failed'. By comparison, when in a combat environment the risks are so much greater that anything afterwards seems insignificant.

Notes

* A pseudonym has been used to protect the identity of the interviewee.
1 See e.g. C. Barrett (2015, December 18), Ups and downs of a stock market rollercoaster year, *Financial Times* Op Ed, accessed at: https://www.ft.com/content/ e161ba86-a4bd-11e5-97e1-a754d5d9538c; T. Cunningham (2016, January 8), Markets stabilise after a rollercoaster start to 2016, *Telegraph*, accessed at: http://www.telegraph.co.uk/finance/markets/ftse100/12088643/Markets-stabilise-after-rollercoaster-start-to-2016.html; 565 point drop in the Dow, Wednesday, January 20, 2016, China's circuit breaker, Iran's sanctions lifted leading to massive volatility in the oil markets (M. Egan (2016, January 20), From horrible to just bad: Dow ends down 249 points, *CNN Money*, accessed at http:// money.cnn.com/2016/01/20/investing/stocks-markets-dow-oil-china/index. html).
2 For instance, Professor John Coates, a leading neuroscientist and former trader, identifies the need to utilise sport science far more efficiently in dealing with trading excesses and irrationality – see the concluding chapter of J. Coates (2012c), *The Hour Between Dog and Wolf: Risk Taking, Gut Feelings, and the Biology of Boom and Bust* (London: Fourth Estate).
3 'Even apart from the instability due to speculation, there is the instability due to the characteristic of human nature that a large proportion of our positive activities depend on spontaneous optimism rather than mathematical expectations, whether moral or hedonistic or economic. Most, probably, of our decisions to do something positive, the full consequences of which will be drawn out over many days to come, can only be taken as the result of animal spirits – a spontaneous urge

to action, and not as the weighted average of quantitative benefits multiplied by quantitative probabilities'. M. Keynes (1936b), *The General Theory of Employment, Interest and Money* (London: Palgrave Macmillan), pp. 161–162.

4 NB. One does not really trade 'money' directly – one trades securities that represent financial assets. Nevertheless, these securities evoke the image, feeling and reality of engaging with money in the brain of a trader who is engaging with the securities.

5 Novelty, or uncertainty, remains a cornerstone feature of the markets.

6 *Herding* refers for instance to following the herd and ending up in a crowded and often unprofitable trade: see Chapter 2 for further explanation.

7 President and Founder of Kynikos Associates.

8 Barclays, for example, recently produced a Cycle of Investor Emotions to help investors cope more effectively with the often emotional and stressful investing process.

2 Money – a love story

> Our brains are identical to the ones which emerged from Africa 100,000 years
> ago. You take a cave man, shave him, give him a 3-piece suit, and put him
> on Wall St., and he looks like all the other barbarians on Wall St. Our brains
> haven't changed at all in the last 100,000 years.
> — Theoretical physicist Michio Kaku (Dabbs, 2000, p. 58)

Gordon Gekko, the fictional Wall Street trader and protagonist of Oliver
Stone's *Wall Street* (1987), said that 'greed, for want of a better word . . . is
good. Greed is right. Greed works. Greed clarifies, cuts through, and cap-
tures the essence of the evolutionary spirit'.

And he was right.

For whilst orthodox economics theories assumed the rationality of man,
we now know that greed – amongst many other powerful emotions –
remains central not only to our evolutionary design, but also to the way that
we trade.

In short, whilst luminaries of behavioural finance and other post-classical
economics disciplines have been able to tells us that we *are* irrational, it is
only evolutionary science that holds the key to understanding *why*. This
chapter subsequently takes the reader on a rip-roaring journey through key
tenets of evolutionary science, the love story that exists between money and
the human mind, the way that each individual's brain chemistry makes him
more statistically likely to commit securities fraud and insider trading and
the way that the financial markets can turn us into gamblers and addicts.
It engages the reader with insights into how, ultimately, the dominance
of our emotional responses in decision-making was designed, in a homo
sapiens' original, natural environment, to be purely rational. The concept
of '*nature vs. the markets*' is a thread that weaves together key theories
and insights throughout the book and explains, ultimately, the fundamental

systemic weakness of the financial markets: that they indulge our emotional impulses, sometimes excessively, whilst pushing back relentlessly – and sometimes overwhelmingly – against our weaker, rational brains.

Money – a love story

We are thoroughly seduced by money, yet its seductive influence remains greatly underestimated; the power of money on the brain is 'a woefully neglected topic' (Furnham, 2006, p. 185) and one that this book strives to offer unique insights into.

To return to Gordon Gekko's wise and entertaining words, greed is defined as an 'intense and selfish desire for something, especially wealth, power, or food'.[1] Greed is the simple emotional manifestation of an early homo sapiens's biological design that drove them, with singular focus, to acquire the objects, nutrients and social positions necessary to ensure the survival on oneself and one's family with 'aggression, fear, protection-seeking and renewed aggressiveness' (Lorenz, 1963, p. 55).

Our brains were (then and now) brilliantly designed to reward us – via an overwhelming flood of dopamine – and to strengthen us – via a rapid influx of testosterone – when we captured prey or faced wild beasts (testosterone enables acts of territorial aggression and dominant behaviour, promotes mating and plays a key role in pursuing social status; Eisenegger et al., 2011). It is a concept, in fact, that we will enjoy returning to many times in this book.

But therein lies the real problem for modern man. Greed is no longer good, particularly in the case of the financial markets. This is because the design of the financial markets and the act of trading itself are both designed to indulge completely the brain's 'reward' system, pumping up our testosterone levels when we excitedly anticipate a trade, flooding our brain with dopamine when we make a trade and semi-permanently pushing up cortisol (our 'stress' hormone) as a result of constant market volatility.

The seduction of money

Hedonism (commonly known as the study of 'pleasure and pain') enjoyed a prominent role as far back as the Ancient Greek-era in defining economic theory. It was only very recently that the logical positivists of the 1930s, in a pursuit of unification of scientific theory, called for an outright rejection of the role of emotion in economics, which led to the recent dominance of *homo economicus* and the idea of rational man in orthodox theory. Whilst we will be discussing this idea at greater length later in the book, one enthralling idea can be invoked here: that money seduces us so immediately and with such strength that this emotion of seduction renders us immediately and permanently unable to trade completely rationally. We can seek to control these emotions, but we cannot deny them. Doing so renders us unable to predict, or understand the true nature of, boom-and-bust scenarios. This book, of course, argues a case for a return to a far greater appreciation of *homo biologicus* (the biology of man).

> Your brain developed to improve our species' odds of survival. You, like every other human, are wired to crave what looks rewarding and shun what seems risky. To counteract these impulses, your brain has only a thin veneer of modern, analytical circuits that are often no match for the power of the ancient parts of your mind.
>
> (Zweig, 2007, p. 3)

As stated so wisely by Albert Einstein, 'not everything that counts can be counted, and not everything that can be counted, counts'.[2] That is certainly true of the markets when it comes to understanding the seductive nature of money. If we wish to understand and predict the markets more effectively, we certainly need to move beyond an exclusive reliance on technical and fundamental analysis of financial and economic data to an appreciation of our emotional impulses when it comes to money's seductive effects.

It has been said that money is the 'desire of desire' (Jorion, quoted in Lea & Webley, 2006, p. 187). It enlivens feelings of admiration, envy and greed in our prehistoric brain: we suffer from 'money illusion' (Weber et al., 2009, p. 5026) and cannot help but be thoroughly, and irrationally, seduced by it.

> The steady drumbeat of stock market gains (the S&P 500 Index closed at record highs on eight different occasions between the election and year-end [2016]) casts a spell on market participants – no-one wants to miss this ticket to paradise.
>
> (Klarman, 1991, p. 4)

Seduction occurs as a result of *greed* – that very essence of the evolutionary spirit that was designed to be a positive – to keep us alive. Commodified and packaged into financial instruments, it becomes something else, and now we are facing an altogether different type of competition: nature versus the markets. Whereas a modern-day trader might be about to trade an ETF in an aggressive (metaphorical) bear market, his Palaeolithic genome may think that that bear is real (at least in terms of the priming effect that it exerts on his body, enabling him to gain the strength to fight – or the speed to run).

Money: the 'desire of desire'

> Stop before a showcase with money in your pocket; the objects displayed are already more than half yours.
>
> — Jean-Paul Sartre (1943 p. 753)

Money, it has been said, literally arouses us (Lea & Webley, 2006). It clouds our rational decision-making capacities and has been referred to as a potentially addictive drug (Lea & Webley, 2006), even when we are simply in its presence (Zink et al., 2004). It is certainly also encouraged by a culture of 'extremes' in many Wall Street banks. Erin Callan, ex-CFO of Lehman Brothers, for example, likened the intensive working culture at Lehman to a 'drug addiction – except you're getting tremendous positive reinforcement for what probably is really extremist behavior' (Kolhatkar, 2013). What Callan is referring to is the idea that a trader can use money as a means of gaining biological incentives/ benefits (e.g. a greater feeling of pleasure via arousal of the limbic system) (Lea & Webley, 2006, p. 161), which can easily lead to addictive and gambling-related behaviours. It is perhaps no surprise, then, that gambling and trading actually do possess similar characteristics. This is partly attributable to the central role given to 'a literal common currency for reward in the brain' (Saxe & Haushofer, 2008, p. 164) in both scenarios – and that common currency is dopamine. This common currency might explain in part the fact that financial rewards are sometimes utilised as a substitute for drugs in treatment programmes for drug addiction (Higgins et al., 2000).

Addicted to trading?

Trading increases dopamine, the 'reward' sensation experienced by the brain when we do something pleasurable. This raises concern regarding gambling and sensation-seeking behaviour engaged in by traders, due in part to the addiction to this dopamine response that it creates. The 'infinite capacities of application' that money creates in our minds renders interactions with money highly emotional (Lea & Webley, 2006, p. 167). Markedly high or low levels of dopamine can immediately interfere with rational thought, as they disrupt working memory. Fewer dopamine receptors have been shown to lead to higher levels of risk-taking activity in teens (Steinberg, 2010), and variances in dopamine levels have been seen to influence financial decision-making amongst college students

(Dreber et al., 2009). A decrease in dopamine receptor 4 gene in the prefrontal cortex is associated with increased novelty seeking, attention deficit hyperactivity disorder and substance abuse, and plays a central role in addiction (Rogers et al., 2004).

A recent example of similarities across trading and gambling environments (see Figure 2.1) can be found in the recent Brexit vote in the UK. Comparing the volatility demonstrated by the European stock index (Euro-STOXX 50) with a gambling index (e.g. Oddschecker) shows us a strong correlation in observed behaviours

Brexit carries significant negative economic outcomes (e.g. a projected loss of up to €1.8 trillion in bank assets), so fundamental data shows that Brexit is a risky proposition. The success of the 'Yes' campaign rested on a sentiment-driven campaign driven by bombastic statements (e.g. '£350m a week we pay to the European Union can instead be spent on the NHS if you vote to Leave'). Whilst the NHS figure was quickly, and subsequently, debunked, Brexit has now entered initial stages of negotiation (Finch, 2017). We can observe in this case that Brexit voting patterns were therefore notably similar in nature to the phenomenon of market sentiment in trading and investing.

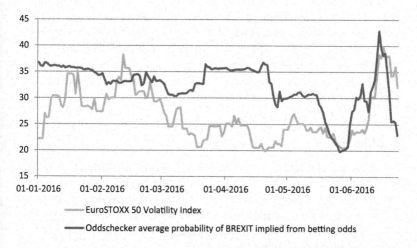

Figure 2.1 EUROSTOXX 50 volatility index vs. Oddschecker BREXIT implied betting odds

'If you're in trouble, double'

'When you're in trouble, double' – a phrase commonly used in trading – mimics the idea of 'doubling down' in gambling – increasing one's financial commitment in a gamble or trade to dial back big losses. The similarity might not only be limited to a shared vocabulary, but to a shared dopaminergic response in pathological gamblers and overly risky traders, and a deficient ventral striatum that handles the monitoring of reward in the brain (Peterson et al., 2010). This can lead to the onset of addictive behaviours and is exacerbated by the constant uncertainty of the markets, which also raise allostatic load (see Figure 1.9). A proclivity for immediate rewards in pathological gamblers even at the cost of longer-term losses (Linnet et al., 2010) is thus a commonly evidenced trait in some traders and gamblers.

Perhaps unsurprisingly, trading (but not investing) has been classified as 'action-oriented gambling' (Pavalko, 2001, p. 34). In fact, sensation seeking as a contributor to trading anomalies is considered so fascinating as to lead to scholars to 'beg for investigation of other arenas where the behavioural attributes [of sensation seeking in trading activity] studied here tend to operate' (Grinblatt & Keloharju, 2009a, p. 574). It might also explain the markedly irrational trading in ETFs and the explosion of the $4 trillion ETF sector over recent years (see 'Exploding ETFs' in Chapter 3).

Research supports the idea that traders might be exposed to the development of gambling tendencies or addictions (e.g. Apicella et al., 2014). These addictions are doubly dangerous as they carry a knock-on effect of potentially exposing traders to a greater vulnerability to engage in fraud (e.g. Jia, 2014), poorer self-regulation (van Honk et al., 2011), financial misreporting (e.g. Baker, 2000 – see 'The face of fraud' later in this chapter) and earnings manipulation (Schrand & Zechman, 2012).

Trading high

For many people, trading provides a high. Where the distinction falls in the life cycle of a trader's career, between the brain's ability to execute rational trades to achieve profit or to simply trade to achieve a dopamine response (i.e. to feed an addiction) (e.g. Goldberg & Lewis, 1978), sometimes becomes hard to discern. It subsequently poses a serious concern in the provocation of gambling addictions:

> behaviour with respect to money is just like behaviour with respect to typical drugs because money is such a reliable tool for getting what the brain is always looking for, namely, relief from boredom. But it isn't

the money itself that is the drug, it is gambling. Money in the gambling addict is – literally – a tool for getting drugged.

(Lea & Webley, 2006, p. 193)

Thrill junkies or risk takers?

Dr Tim Fong, Co-Director of the UCLA Gambling Studies Program, notes that pathological gamblers exhibit certain dysfunctions which are present prior to addiction, which tells us that some populations are more vulnerable to addiction that others (Fong, 2005). Some traders are also what some might call 'thrill junkies' – energetic, risk-taking, high-testosterone. As Bloomberg News Editor Depew notes, long-term exposure to the financial markets can bring out the worst, as opposed to the best, in these traits:

> Thrill junkies choose gambling for the intensity of the experience, and behavioural psychology long ago demonstrated that the mind's ability to choose rational thrills offering positive rewards over more intense thrills offering irrational, negative rewards is pitiful at best. We're simply not wired that way.
>
> (Dorn, 2014)

Elevated levels of neurotransmitters can be a signifying factor in problem or pathological gamblers (Paris et al., 2010) (attributable to HPA hypo-arousal in response to gambling cues). A culmination of these physiological effects may explain why the average portfolio turnover for a retail investor over one (annualised) quarter is 75%, rising in some cases to 250% (Barber & Odean, 2000). In other words, retail investors seem to endemically over-trade. Whatever the reason for this turnover, it is certainly not profit: the most over-active groups underperform the wider markets by around 6% (Dorn & Sengmueller, 2009). It might instead be explained by gambling tendencies and a simple enjoyment of the gambling-esque act of placing a trade over and over.

This kind of 'entertainment effect' (Dorn & Sengmueller, 2009, p. 592; (Zuckerman, 1994) shows us that trading may simply represent a hobby for many retail (Main Street) investors. As such, they trade primarily for fun and not profit (Anderson, 2008; Dorn & Sengmueller, 2009): 'Our results suggest that many private investors may simply enjoy trading and focus more on the thrill and less on the profit' (Markiewicz & Weber, 2013, p. 76).

For some retail investors, for whom trading really is simply a hobby (Goetzmann & Dhar, 2004), and where realisation utility may be wholly non-pecuniary (i.e. not economic) (e.g. Barberis & Xiong, 2008), trading may subsequently become unprofitable and 'hazardous to the investors' wealth' (Dorn & Sengmueller, 2009, p. 602). It also makes the markets far more unpredictable.

Animal spirits

In January 2017, following President Donald Trump's inauguration, Seth Klarman (a highly regarded value investor and CEO of hedge fund Baupost), commented that 'ensuing animal spirits drove US stocks to repeated new highs' (Klarman, 2017, p. 3). Klarman also commented on the fact that 'the S&P 500 recently traded at the 85th percentile of its historical valuation over the last 40 years', citing how the election had 'cast a spell on market participants – no-one wants to miss this ticket to paradise' (Klarman, 2017, p. 4).

What does this mean? Well, Klarman's observations of bewitched traders and investors, and animal spirits (ibid., p. 161) echoed pertinently the famous words of John Maynard Keynes, who first remarked that individuals are driven by 'animal spirits', or spontaneous optimism (Keynes, 1936a), as opposed to a rational analysis of fundamental market values. 'Animal spirits' refers to the 'spontaneous urge to action rather than inaction, and not as the outcome of a weighted average of quantitative benefits' in one's investing decisions (Keynes, 2007, p. 161).

Keynes remains a foundational influence in the field of economics, with Nobel-prize winner George Akerlof (2003) citing Keynes as having made the 'greatest contribution to behavioural economics before the present era' (Andruszliewicz et al., 2013, p. 147). Andruszliewicz et al. (2013) go as far as to suggest that 'animal spirits' of the kind advocated by Keynes should perhaps be included as a 'hidden variable' (p. 164) in economic theorisations, reflecting the notion that emotions such as optimism or pessimism are relatively enduring states.

It is within this context that the illuminating field of behavioural finance has emerged – a field of study that has been referred to as 'perhaps the most important conceptual innovation in economics over the last thirty years' (Shleifer, 2012, p. 1), with its rapid rise attributable to 'its sharp, testable predictions and wide availability of data contradicting the efficient markets hypothesis, thereby showing that arbitrage, learning, and evolution do not eliminate human limitations and complications' (Sent, 2004, p. 749). It can be defined as the analysis of what happens when agents fail to act rationally, fail to incorporate new information into their behaviour, or make choices that are not rationally consistent with maximising expected utility (Barberis & Thaler, 2002, p. 2). It counters the argument of Friedman (1953),

which assumes that rational traders will quickly void the market disloca-
tions caused by irrational traders.

Howard Marks (2014), CEO of Oaktree Capital Group (one of the world's
largest distressed debt investors) remarked, in a 2014 internal memo to clients, that 'the probability of loss is no more measurable than the probability of rain' and that risk cannot, consequently, be quantified *a priori*. This
reflects an ideological shift 'toward developing models of human psychology as it relates to financial markets' (Shiller, 2003, p. 90). Drawing heavily
on cognitive psychology (e.g. Camerer, 1995; Rabin, 1998; Kahneman et
al., 1982; Kahneman & Tversky, 2000; Gilovich et al., 2002), behavioural
finance identifies how beliefs and cognitive bias such as over-confidence,
optimism, representativeness, conservatism, belief perseverance, anchoring
and availability can lead to non-rational trading and investing.

In recent years, the emergence of neuroscience has added significant
insight into the field (often referred to as neuroeconomics or neurofinance;
e.g. Zak, 2004). By way of a brief introduction, neuroeconomics combines
the fields of economics, neuroscience and psychology to determine how
individuals make economic choices and decisions. Many neuroeconomic
and neurofinance studies now utilise fMRI (functional magnetic resonance
imaging) technologies, which offer a sophisticated means of studying the
brain in economic decision-making. Neurofinance has offered many exciting observations, such as the fact that overstimulating the parts of the brain
that are activated by financial decision-making (particularly the amygdala,
the nucleus accumbens and the anterior insula) can cause irrational behaviour and may 'exacerbate financial difficulties into a crisis' (Manesidis,
2013, p. 41).

The key role of neurotransmitters (e.g. serotonin, dopamine), alongside
hormones such as testosterone, oxytocin, vasopressin, and cortisol have
been observed to play a significant part in moderating risk preferences.
Cortisol levels of derivatives and options traders, for example, were found
to correlate with the implied volatility of German treasury bonds in one
experiment (Hennessey & Levine, 1979), and oxytocin levels stimulated a
desire for in-group conformity (Stallen et al., 2012). Testosterone causes a
'winner effect' that can lead to over-confident trading and long-term losses
(Dufty, 1989), whilst males with high testosterone have been found to be
more likely to seek to exploit others in their quest for status (Manesidis,
2013) – as well as being less financially generous (Zak et al., 2009).

These fields of study are fascinating and complex. It is not possible as
a result to truly do them justice here.[3] However, an introduction is certainly achievable, as is a contextualisation of behavioural finance theory
in the wider context of 'animal spirits', which has been provided here. As

Thorstein Veblen (1898) noted as far back as 1898, 'economics, properly understood, is simply a branch of biology'. It is perhaps no surprise, in that context, that behavioural finance and the role of biology in economic decision-making are consequently enjoying a return.

We can consider irrationality to be any

> thought, emotion or behaviour that leads to self-defeating consequences or that significantly interferes with the survival and happiness of the organism. . . [that] often seem to flow from deep-seated and almost ineradicable tendencies toward human fallibility, overgeneralization, wishful thinking, gullibility, prejudice, and short-range hedonism; and they appear at least in part tied up with physiological, hereditary, and constitutional processes,
>
> (Ellis, 1975, p. 3)

and it is to these irrationalities, in the form of observations made by behavioural finance experts, that we shall now turn.

The winner effect

The experience of winning can lead to a 40% increase in testosterone (Carré & Putnam, 2010), which in turn leads to a surge of dopamine (the brain's 'reward' neurotransmitter). Testosterone can remain elevated for days or even weeks afterward (ibid.). Baseline testosterone levels may reflect a personality trait, if one observes the literature relating to testosterone and power, social status and dominance (Eisenegger et al., 2011), with testosterone levels increasing in anticipation of either physical or non-physical competition (ibid., p. 265) and reducing one's fear so that one experiences greater confidence to act. Testosterone downregulates our hypothalamic–pituitary–adrenal stress response (Hermans et al., 2006), so in the short term it can actually prove beneficial, but can cause overly risky trading over longer periods. In a study of Rhesus monkeys, for example, testosterone levels were found to be ten times higher in winning monkeys in a competition for rank and status, with a 10% baseline level of testosterone observed in the losing monkeys (Monaghan & Glickman, 2001).

Traders might well appear to have higher testosterone levels than the general population, given the necessity of the vocation to readily take on risk, often under considerable pressure. On the face of it, this is logical, give its effect on risk taking: 'men who fought and hunted in dangerous primitive environments needed to focus on the task and move quickly with confidence and optimism' (Dabbs & Dabbs, 2000, pp. 42–43). But, as the reader will see throughout the pages of this book, it also carries a significant downside.

House money effect

The house money effect refers to the tendency for investors and traders to be more likely to buy higher-risk stocks after execution of a profitable trade, because they mentally separate existing capital from recent profits, and view these recent profits as disposable.

Androgenic priming

Another related and equally compelling concept is the so-called challenge effect (Eisenegger et al., 2011), where testosterone rises in the context of a perceived challenge, priming us for action and increasing territorial dominance. A great sporting analogy can be found in the sport of American football – recently, the Dallas Cowboys hired an 'intimidation coach' (Bupp, 2016), whose specific remit was to prime Cowboys players to intimidate, and to not be intimidated by, rival athletes. This approach capitalises on the endogenous rise of testosterone that is experienced in the face of a challenge (the so-called challenge hypothesis; Coates et al., 2010).

The anticipatory effect/challenge effect

Respected economist W. S. Jevons, quoted as far back as 1888,[4] wrote that the

> power of anticipation must have a large influence in Economics; for upon it is based all accumulation of stocks of commodity to be consumed at a future time. That class or race of men who have the most foresight will work most for the future. The untutored savage, like the child, is wholly occupied with the pleasures and the troubles of the moment; the morrow is dimly felt; the limit of his horizon is but a few days off. The wants of a future year, or of a lifetime, are wholly unforeseen.
>
> (Jevons, 1888, p. 28)

Interestingly, it is not only achievement of a goal, but anticipating that goal, that really innervates us. Financial risk taking behaviours (i.e. trading decisions) can be altered in the presence of 'incidental reward cues' – e.g. a charismatic broker using charm, and the 'reward' cue of images of superyachts and Lamborghinis in their marketing. These reward cues significantly ramp up the valence of the reward and thus also neurologically impact the power of the anticipatory effect, motivating us to act so that reward is achieved. This is due to a 'neuropsychological mechanism that may underlie effective emotional appeals' (Knutson et al., 2008, p. 2), such as a rise in dopamine and a rise in testosterone (Apicella et al., 2008) that are triggered by emotionally satisfying appeals (e.g. the superyacht, the ego-boosting effect of a charismatic, charming broker on our ego).

> For people who trade because they like to do so, the monetary cost of trading is offset by non-pecuniary benefits from researching, executing, talking about, and anticipating the outcome of, or experiencing the outcome of a trade.
>
> (Black, 1986, p. 531)

The powerful and excitatory effects of anticipation can also be effectively amplified by external variables (Loewenstein et al., 2001) such as media headlines, 'fake news' or Twitter announcements. Savvy financial news providers are adept at leveraging this neural response to sell more newspapers,[5] which feeds into our need for anticipating a new, exciting story, but can then cloud our judgement in making trading and investing decisions.

The framing effect

The dominance of the amygdala (a region of the brain) in the decision-making process of a trader plays a central role in the 'framing effect' (referred to as 'a deviation from rational decision-making': De Martino et al., 2009, p. 684) or, in other words, the likelihood that a trader would become too risk-averse or too pro-risk as a result of the strength of his amygdala activation. Whilst it has been acknowledged that 'in evolutionary terms, this mechanism may confer a strong advantage . . . in modern society . . . such mechanisms may render human choices irrational' (De Martino et al., 2009, pp. 3–4).

Investors often deviate significantly from predicted behaviours (e.g. Schleifer, 2012, p. 2; Bénabou, 2013, p. 451). These authors, for example, identify wilful blindness in the form of *ex ante* information avoidance (not wanting to know), and *ex post* belief distortion (reality denial); note the power of the social transmission of beliefs, where wilful ignorance is contagious (also see 'Excitation transfer' later in this section).

We can also be persuaded by 'gatekeepers' to wealth – e.g. the aforementioned charismatic broker who seemingly possesses the key to wealth and status – to alter our opinion from rational to risky based on the strength and valence of emotional appeals that they make, and because of how our brains reward us with a surge in dopamine and testosterone when we hear and enjoy those appeals. This can lead often to a wilful avoidance of data in favour of charismatic rhetoric and seductive promises. This is often discussed in behavioural finance literature as a 'framing effect' – 'a striking violation of standard economic accounts of human rationality' (De Martino et al., 2009, p. 684).

The charisma/gatekeeper effect

A pervasive 'financial porn' culture plays on our evolutionary design, offering a 24/7 stream of financial news (of varying accuracy and quality) to gain advertising dollars and compete in a saturated media market. To gain traction in the news sector, soundbites and headlines have become increasingly sensationalistic, glossy, attention-grabbing and/or reassuring, offering (purportedly sage but often poor) investing advice in a turbulent market to settle addled nerves and insecure investors. We seem far more vulnerable to the voices of charismatic brokers in volatile markets, as they offer us security and reassurance and represent gatekeepers to wealth. But is following a charismatic, reassuring voice sensible? Turning to research: 'In evolutionary terms, this mechanism may confer a strong advantage. . . [but] such mechanisms may render human choices irrational' (De Martino et al., 2009, p. 684). This is, as research indicates, not usually a wise approach to adopt. Charisma as a trait is amoral and is often actually linked to narcissism (see page 70, 'Big Men, Big Lies,' for further explanation), with observations of its power leading to negative, as well as positive, outcomes:

> If your company is heading in the right direction, a charismatic leader will get you there faster. Unfortunately, if you're heading in the wrong direction, charisma will also get you there faster.
>
> (Stadler & Dyer, 2013)

Anchoring and cognitive dissonance

Some people possess the tendency to 'promulgate therapeutic orthodoxies and excoriate and excommunicate apostates that deviate from their dogmas' (Ellis, 1975, p. 25), simply because we are hardwired to seek reassurance and would rather feel reassured than right. Anchoring therefore reflects the tendency of a person to be overly influenced by the first piece of information they encounter, with cognitive dissonance reflecting their subsequent inability to change this belief in the context of new, high-quality but conflicting information.

A great example is represented in the moment when Alan Greenspan was told that a number of investors, including Michael Burry, CEO of Scion Capital, had been able to predict the 2008 financial crisis, when the Federal Reserve had failed to do so. Greenspan remained unable to admit his mistakes. His response? 'There's a group, a relatively small but not negligible group, who got it mostly by luck' (Comstock, 2010). Greenspan was simply unable to admit that he had been wrong, or that some others – using different methods than his own – had been right.

Bias

There are many types of bias: status quo bias (taking bigger gambles to maintain the status quo), confirmation bias (seeking out data that confirms our position, reacting differently to confirmatory and non-confirmatory data after having formed an opinion), hindsight bias (over-estimating one's ability to predict future events) and self-attribution bias (attributing success to one's own actions, and failures to external sources: 'we will consistently overrate our abilities, particularly in areas that are completely outside of our circle of competence'; Sinclair, 2013, p. 154).

A proclivity in choosing domestic equities (French & Poterba, 1991) over non-domestic ones, for example, constitutes a *home bias*, whilst positive feedback trading (Barberis & Shleifer, 2003) refers to a tendency to attribute too much value to stock that recently demonstrated an upward momentum, leading to the over-purchasing of stock. Barber and Odean (2001) found, for example, that the more people traded, the more they lost, representing a tendency for over-optimism (also see Daniel et al., 1998, 2001).

Representativeness and availability heuristic

Traders and investors often display a tendency to make decisions based on the first piece of evidence that they come across (a heuristic, or 'rule of thumb'). This represents a potentially dangerous tendency: 'While calculating correct probabilities can be easy for those who know the appropriate rules of thumb and historical trends, traders who have not learned the valid shortcuts will naturally use the invalid ones' (Sinclair, 2013, p. 155).

A *representativeness heuristic*,[6] for example, explains a tendency to expect the continuance of stock returns relative to recent performance, especially if similar assets have retained an upward momentum (Shleifer, 2012) (e.g. the US housing bubble that burst in 2007). Schiller (2000, p. xii, cited in Thompson, 2014, p. 94) observed that this kind of heuristic represents an irrational 'wishful thinking on the parts of investors that blinds us to the truth of the real situation'. It is irrational – and potentially damaging – because it leads to 'anomalous and persistent stock price movements that are not correlated in any discernible way with underlying asset values', contributing to the earlier cited 'positive feedback trading' (Thompson, 2014, p. 94). As stated well by Hyman Minsky: 'Financing is often based on an assumption 'that the existing state of affairs will continue indefinitely' (Keynes, 1936a, p. 152); an assumption that is often proven to be blindingly incorrect.

Over-optimism

Over-optimism (i.e. an unfounded and overly positive belief in the price or performance of an asset) can lead to excessive takeover activity by CEOs (Roll, 1986) and the emergence of unusual trading patterns or decisions (such as the over-purchase of a stock when the price is rising).

Belief perseverance

Belief perseverance and the *sunken costs fallacy* explain an investor's dogmatic approach to persevere with a particular course of action, even though it is beginning to show signs of danger or unacceptable risk (e.g. doubling down on a trade to recoup earlier losses).

Herding and cognitive dissonance

As noted by Seth Klarman, author of *Margin of Safety* and CEO of Baupost,

> It is always easiest to run with the herd; at times, it can take a deep reservoir of courage and conviction to stand apart from it. Yet distancing yourself from the crowd is an essential component of long-term investment success.

What Klarman is referring to here is 'herding'. In other words, 'the mass psychological aspect of trend formation is related to herding impulses involved in the limbic system, the part of the brain that involves emotions and motivation' (Cymbalista, 2003, p. 32).

How can we be rational if we are hardwired, biologically, to act on emotions, not logic, in order to ensure our survival? It has been said that 'in making short-term predictions, neural systems tap into gut feelings and emotions' (Blakeslee, 2003), and one such gut feeling, or emotion, is the strong evolutionary urge to belong, and the sensation of actual pain when we buck the consensus, regardless of how sensible that decision might be. Returning to the earlier-quoted bucking-the-trend issue:

> when people did buck the consensus, brain scans found intense firing in the amygdala. Neuroscientist Gregory Berns, who led the study, calls this flare up a sign of 'the emotional lead associated with standing up

for one's belief' . . . In short, you go along with the herd not because
you want to, but because it hurts not to.

(Zweig, 2007, p. 109)

Herding may be attributable to an amplification of already higher-than-
average testosterone levels on a trading floor, where individuals, already
confident in taking risks and perhaps prone to over-confidence, experience further pleasure (via a surge in dopamine) in acting in a group,
regardless of how sensible that decision might ultimately prove: 'The
total group effects of testosterone may be more than the sum of the
effects in all the individuals separately' (Dabbs, 2000, p. 84) (see 'Excitation transfer' on p. 53).

This might explain the feeling of overly 'alpha' behaviour or 'too much
testosterone' on all-male trading floors, or difficulties in whistleblowing,
given the way the brain often experiences pleasure when we observe a punishment of outsiders who contradict social norms (de Quervain et al., 2004).
An added danger is the fact that traders and investors may act as a herd so
that they do not risk underperforming colleagues (a risk that might get them
fired). It might also reflect excessively short-term pressures to make profits
for their clients ('they have their own dire needs for their clients' approval
and frequently tie these clients to them in an extended dependency relationship'; Ellis, 1975, p. 25).

Herding represents that urge to belong to, and act as, a group. Social
status, social rewards and money all actually receive the same 'reward' currency in the brain (Saxe & Haushofer, 2008): 'Your dopamine system plays
off my dopamine system. You buy, I buy, I worry about you, our systems
become entrained. You sell, I sell' (Montague, 2007, p. 3). There appears,
in fact, to be 'a substantial overlap between the neural representation of
monetary and social reward' (Saxe & Haushofer, 2008, p. 164) with social
acceptance producing the same neural rewards in the brain as money. Money
can buy a more sophisticated social standing in the community – an allur-
ing idea for some (Lea & Webley, p. 164), also offering an 'an indicator of
achievement, respect, and freedom or power' (Lea & Webley, 2006, p. 179).

In summary, homo sapiens are hardwired to act in social groups. We
experience 'drug-like changes in human biochemistry after changes in
status' (Mazur & Booth, 1998), with status often comprising the 'reward'
that we attain for winning group approval. Perhaps some people become
addicted to the social cache that trading, or achieving big profitable trades,
affords them. The factors discussed here thus explain why there are observable neural causes for the phenomenon of herding in the financial markets
(Thaler, 1991; Blasco et al., 2012).

Excitation transfer

Excitation-transfer theory explains how the body's excitatory response (i.e. how we become 'excited') is amplified via exposure to others' emotions and powerful outside stimuli (e.g. Twitter feeds, Bloomberg reports, 'fake news'). This heightens the dangers of experiencing market sentiment-led activity as a result of excitatory-transfer of emotions such as anger, fear, over-optimism and panic, which can lead to a major motivation to trade emotionally and irrationally (Bryant & Miron, 2003; Zillmann, 1998).

> Residual excitation from essentially any excited emotional reaction is capable of intensifying any other excited emotional reaction. The degree of intensification depends, of course, on the magnitude of residues prevailing at the time.
>
> (Zillmann, 2006, p. 223)

Donald Trump's now-infamous wiretap tweet on March 4, 2017 may demonstrate this idea well ('How low has President Obama gone to tapp my phones during the very sacred election process. This is Nixon/Watergate. Bad (or sick) guy!'). Trump allegedly wrote the tweet straight after viewing an alt-right report about wiretapping, and excitatory-transfer seems to have taken place between TV commentator and president (given the absence of fact-checking, the timing of the tweet, and the basic spelling error – 'tapp'). This response is indicative of how powerful such a transfer can be, and how it can over-ride our ability to effectively control our impulses.

Churning and overtrading

It has been remarked that 'the high trading volume on organized exchanges is perhaps the single most embarrassing fact to the standard finance paradigm' (De Bondt & Thaler, 1995, p. 392). It is a remark that reflects the role of emotion in over-trading, which leads regularly to unprofitable trading and contributes to market fragility and volatility. This is a phenomenon also known as 'churning' – the tendency to over-trade, which can also be attributed to *short-term thinking* (Gore & Blood, 2009).

Hot money

Animal spirits are amplified and, perhaps, manipulated by external sources. One such notable source is the media, to which this chapter now turns.

A golden age of ignorance?

'We live in a golden age of ignorance', according to Robert Proctor, a historian who created the word 'agnotology' to explain the deliberate production of ignorance (Harford, 2017, p. 14; Proctor's insights correlated well with 'post-truth' becoming the Oxford Dictionaries word of 2016). As Tim Harford, a *Financial Times* journalist, economist and former BBC radio fact checker, notes, 'The facts need a champion' (2017, p. 18). The conscious creation and dissemination of lies via mass media has become something of an art, with Brexit and the Trump presidency offering examples in the use of mass extrapolation of misleading data. Proctor comments: 'Fact checkers can become Trump's poodle, running around like an errand boy checking someone else's facts. If all your time is [spent] checking someone else's facts, then what are you doing?' (ibid., p. 16).

It is a valid question and one that holds a stark reality for both retail and institutional investors. Termed 'financial porn' by Emmy-award winning writer Jane Bryant Quinn, the explosion in 24/7 cable news networks, internet investing sites, investing manuals and spam muddies the waters for investors, promoting confusion and irrationality.

There are numerous examples of hot money stories flooding the market – e.g. 'most of this flow-surge is Trump inspired hot money looking for a quick buck' (Shilling, 2016) – and the phenomenon seems to span, most prolifically, the years enveloping the emergence of social media. Take, for example, an August 13, 2013 tweet by legendary investor Carl Icahn: 'We currently have a large position in APPLE. We believe the company to be extremely undervalued. Spoke to Tim Cook today'. The effect of that tweet was monumental, with Apple closing that day with a $12.5bn market capitalization.

Similarly, Elon Musk's August 23, 2016 tweet regarding an imminent product announcement raised Tesla's stock market valuation by $670 million (Charlton, 2016). Donald Trump's biotech and aeronautical tweets have also been very powerful in their effects: it was reported by Kristian Rouz that 'Trump wipe[d] $24.6 bln off drug and biotech stocks in 20 minutes' simply by tweeting (Rouz, 2017). Similarly, Lockheed Martin had over $4 billion wiped from its market capitalisation the same day (December 12, 2016) that President Trump tweeted 'The F-35 program and cost is out of control. Billions of dollars can and will be saved on military (and other) purchases after January 20th' (Thielman, 2006).

The demand for instant communication is such that Goldman Sachs now release their quarterly results via Twitter. The Bank of England, the Central Bank and the US Federal Reserve are also prolific users. JP Morgan's *Global Quantitative and Derivatives Feb 2017 Strategy Report* recently noted that 'information is created and consumed at a much faster pace than e.g. a decade ago, (think of twitter, smartphones, etc.) An emerging class of fully automated quant strategies is also likely to speed up the market reaction' (Kolanovic & Kaplan, 2017, p. 4), with reaction times for large-scale events, such as Brexit, compressed into hours instead of weeks as would previously have been the case.

A glitch in the matrix

A recent paper entitled *The Kinks of Financial Journalism* (Garcia, 2014) reported that over a hundred-year period (1905–2005), journalists displayed a negative bias in reporting. The bias was attributed to a classic irrational behaviour – *loss aversion* – which had either created a demand-led tendency for journalists to tell readers what they wanted to hear, or a supply-led 'hype' designed solely to sell newspapers. As Veldkamp (2005, p. 19) recently noted: 'The reason the *Financial Times* stops reporting obscure information is that they must provide high-demand information to remain profitable'. It is a pressure shared by many in the media world and it does not seem likely to wane any time soon. It also risks creating the kind of bias that leads to excessive yet unconscious irrationality:

> Most people probably do not consider arousal from media exposure to be pronounced enough to warrant any attention, and hence they do not expect it to affect their behavior. Dismissing such arousals as trivial, the individual will tend to attribute any accumulating residues not to the preceding communication events [which are, in this instance, mediated messages] but to the new stimulus situations in which he finds himself. Moreover, by virtue of their very 'unreal' and symbolic (possibly-fantasy encouraging) content, communication messages are generally not related to the person's real and immediate problems and concerns. This should . . . make the person all the more vulnerable to transfer effects in his post-communication behavior.
>
> (Tannenbaum & Zillmann, 1975, p. 187)

It is this kind of fantasy reality that led hedge fund manager David Einhorn to comment in May 2017 that 'investors remain hypnotized by Tesla's CEO. We are sceptical that the company will be able to . . . justify the current valuation'. Einhorn likened the optimism surrounding Tesla to that of the dotcom bubble, and many leading value investors now voice similar concerns, yet Tesla's stock remains hot, particularly amongst retail investors, with an astonishing recent rise in share price so high that Tesla's market capitalisation exceeded that of auto giants General Motors Co. and Ford Motor Co. It is a rise in value based on fantasy and impressive media hype, because it cannot – simply put – be based on fundamental data.

From Wall Street to Washington

This kind of fantasy reality also exerts a profound effect on partisan politics, with brain scans of partisan voters demonstrating engagement of emotional, not rational, brain centres when they viewed or listened to their preferred political candidates:

> None of the circuits involved in conscious reasoning were particularly engaged. Essentially, it appears as if partisans twirl the cognitive kaleidoscope until they get the conclusions they want . . . Everyone from executives and judges to scientists and politicians may reason to emotionally biased judgements when they have a vested interest in how to interpret 'the facts'.
>
> Drew Westen, Director of Clinical Psychology at Emory University
> (Shermer, 2006)

It is certainly not a new premise: as far back as 1620, and long before brain scans were invented, Francis Bacon noted that when we have formed an opinion, facts to the contrary are deemed ignoble variables that the brain 'either neglects and despises . . . in order that by this great and pernicious predetermination the authority of its former conclusions may remain inviolate' (Shermer, 2006).

Westen et al.'s (2006) scientific observations were able to add empirical weight to observations such as Bacon's, finding that Republican and Democrat partisan voters both processed data emotionally, not rationally when faced with clearly contradictory statements made by the leaders of their respective parties. Their brain activity reflected negative affect – in other words, an internal battle to reconcile 'belief' (e.g. I love my party) with 'fact' (my party is flawed).

It is interesting in this context that our brains reward us when we engage in 'forgivability of an action' – in other words, we experience a sensation of pleasure when we find a way to reconcile our desired belief with reality (often requiring a 'lie' to ourselves, or becoming wilfully blind) (Westen et al., 2006, p. 1956). MRI scans in the same study also suggested the experiencing of a frisson of *schadenfreude* when political rivals were seen to contradict themselves, which changed to activity in emotional processing areas associated with tempering a conflict between 'data and desire' (ibid., p. 1951) when viewing our own candidate.

For partisan voters, therefore, voting seems to be a primarily emotional affair, where motivated judgements are 'doubly reinforcing' (Westen et al., 2006, p. 1956). As we have already seen, our brain first seeks to strengthen its belief by avoiding dissonance (the earlier noted 'avoidant and escape conditioning' Westen et al., 2006, p. 1956) and to instead seek out 'emotionally preferable conclusions' (Westen et al., 2006), which our brain then rewards us for (Rada et al., 1998). Irrational voting of this nature can carry serious implications for polarisation of the electorate, and voting that does not result in the best outcomes for a nation state. It was exactly this concern that led to George Washington warning of the dangers of a two-party state that might pit voters against each other in an 'alternate domination of one faction over another, sharpened by the spirit of revenge, natural to party dissension, which in different ages and countries has perpetrated the most horrid enormities, is itself a frightful despotism'. He spoke of 'ill-founded jealousies and false alarms' and – most compellingly in the context of the current FBI investigation into Russian meddling in the US presidential elections – of the dangers of a two-party state in opening 'the door to foreign influence and corruption, which find a facilitated access to the government itself through the channels of party passions'.

Is behavioural finance horseshit?

Former Bear Stearns CEO Ace Greenberg once said that: 'behavioural finance is horseshit'. Physiology, as it turns out, tells us otherwise.

Instead of assaulting these new fields of study, it would be preferable to turn back to evolutionary science, a field which maintains that the 'basic framework for physiologic gene regulation was selected during an era of obligatory physical activity, as the survival of our Late Palaeolithic (50,000–10,000 BC) depended on hunting and gathering' (Booth et al., 2002, p. 399). This subsequently shines a light on the importance of recognising how well we are suited to our environments, how our physiology reacts to money and hyper-stimulation, how we are hardwired to be emotional, not rational, and how, in many ways, we need to regulate against human behaviour because – in the face of the seductive effects of money – it becomes something that we can no longer necessarily control.

Trader physiology: key takeaways

- Money seduces us much like cocaine or falling in love. It could be considered a drug, so arguably it is not possible for anyone to trade or invest completely rationally. Conceptualising investors and traders as *homo biologicus* as opposed to *homo economicus* – for reasons such as this one – would allow us to better face the reality of our physiological reactions to the financial markets;
- Animal spirits and behavioural finance tell us how we trade irrationally – but physiology tells us why – and the latter should constitute a central focus when analysing these irrational, emotional behaviours (e.g. loss aversion, cognitive dissonance, herding, euphoria). This offers a really empowering route to managing destructive impulses;

- There appears to be a fundamental mismatch between our evolutionary design and the indulgent, unpredictable nature of the financial markets which can, for example, trigger addictions and encourage short-termism;
- Traders are hired for their ability to take on risk (which means they are likely to possess higher basal and/or reactive testosterone than many non-traders). Whilst the upside (making profit) is encouraged, the downside (greater potential vulnerability to instincts to trade opportunistically, overly risky trading) is not managed out sufficiently by many financial institutions;
- Testosterone has been linked to fraud, and high testosterone levels, raised as a result of successful trades, can potentially make a trader become overly likely to take on too much risk;
- We are evolutionarily designed to follow charismatic, high-testosterone leaders, particularly when we feel uncertain or insecure (e.g. charismatic broker, finance guru). The physiology of charisma can include a boost in testosterone when we hear the leader speak, and a 'switching off' of the executive function of the brain when we listen to them. Subsequently, charisma could be conceptualised as a physiological process, which leads to emotional, rather than rational, outcomes. These leaders are, unfortunately, often unethical, leading to a potential for a normalisation of fraud and unethical activity.

Special feature: 'the common denominator for fraud is opportunity'

Jeffrey Klink, a recognised expert on financial fraud, is the CEO of Klink & Co., a global risk consultancy that operates across 100 countries. He is a former United States Department of Justice prosecutor and has appeared on a wide range of media outlets in his expert capacity as a fraud specialist, including the Bloomberg network, Fox and ABC.

Q. Why do you think that financial crime is so prevalent in trading and investing?

My experience as a prosecutor and of the professional consulting side is that fraud is deeply entrenched in Wall Street, but it is also deeply entrenched throughout the broader economy. But traders have much greater financial incentives. The problems are bigger, candidly, on Wall Street, because there is more money.

In manufacturing, you might literally see a couple of hundred million dollars kickback scheme, and that would be a very large, large, fraud loss. On Wall Street, traders can make unGodly amounts of money – so they do. And business is structured in such a way that you can get away with fraud.

These kinds of issues are endemic throughout business, so when I hear that people want to deregulate the market (e.g. repealing Dodd–Frank), I know that many people are forgetting that those regulations have come into play as a *direct consequence* of these kinds of bad activities. Think how badly deregulation played out in 2008.

Q. So it is effectively a case of having to regulate against human nature?

Yes . . . the research is very clear – from organisations such as the Association of Certified Fraud Examiners and other reputable long standing research – that the common denominator for fraud is opportunity.

It is simply opportunity.

So, if internal company controls are not good, people are going to find a way to steal, and to defraud. Simply because they can.

Obviously, the pot of money on Wall Street is bigger, and then people try to find out ways to 'beat the system'. And frauds on Wall Street play an outsize role in the economy in terms of the impact they can exert on pension funds, individual investors, and generally confidence in the entire economy. If one business goes down, people notice, but when you see massive disruptions in the markets, it impacts every industry. People worry – should I invest, should I reduce head counts, that kind of thing. The impact is massive.

Q. As a former prosecutor, do you feel that perpetrators of fraud shared any similar characteristics?

I think some of the things I've seen you write about (see Zehndorfer, 2015) have resonance with me. Traits I see are arrogance, and a general thought that workplace rules, relating to conduct, do not seem to apply to these folks. They seem to think they are above it all.

One of the common themes I've seen in fraud cases is that the bad guys have often been acting inappropriately in other non-financial ways throughout their career, but they were viewed as 'successful salesmen' or 'successful managers' so nobody intervened.

I'll give you an interesting story. There was a US steel company that asked a high-ranking executive to sell a business unit worth a few million dollars. This individual sold the unit to a corporate entity that he himself created, and sold it for much less than the value of the business. He'd exhibited some very peculiar traits throughout his career, but because he always made his sales goals, they loved him. If he didn't like how his subordinates were performing – and this is no exaggeration – he would spit on them. In the workplace. And they let him do it.

And these are the guys who often have multiple extra-marital affairs, and just generally don't play by the rules of the road. But because businesses are evaluated on a quarterly cycle – 'I gotta meet my numbers' – people ignore these kinds of behaviours.

Generally, it's a feeling of superiority, and 'the rules don't apply to me and I'm going to get away with this'. The history of financial fraud is replete with cases like that, like the Tyco International CEO, Dennis Kozlowski, spending millions of dollars on bathroom fixtures because he feels like it, and thinks he is going to get away with it. In small fraud cases, you frequently see some personal disarray – gambling, alcohol, dysfunctional home life – those kinds of things.

Q. Do you think that money can make people irrational to the point where they commit financial crime?

Certainly, I think that people become irrational in matters of money.

In many ways, money is a drug. If you've ever been to a casino with someone that lets it get away from them, it is not rational. It is not rational to put $1k down on black. So when you are sitting on a trading terminal, looking at the screen and facing the possibility of a $10m bonus, people, I think, act irrationally.

Before the 2008 crisis some people were doing crazy things, making really, really irrational, crazy investments, simply because the upside was so, so high. I didn't see a lot of those people as irrational, generally, but it felt like people just got captured by the moment. And it seemed like, just before the meltdown, everyone was getting richer and richer. So yes, money is just like an intoxicant.

And I think the reason why some people got to the positions that they reached was simply because they were willing to take big risks. And trading desks could have made more than they ever lost, but they didn't – because they were so irrational.

Q. Do you think that Wall Street and financial institution CEOs and top traders sometimes feel pressured into unethical activities to keep up with competitors?

Yes, absolutely. There is a natural tendency for all of us to measure ourselves against others, and I think that in trading, there is no doubt that people measure themselves against the competition. Essentially, Wall Street is a very small world so when you see a guy making $40m and you are making $20m you think 'hey, I should be making $40m too'.

So I don't want to say that people feel pressured by it, but I think they measure themselves by it. And the expectations of the analysts on Wall Street are not realistic. They are not healthy.

And the way the world of many public companies operate – in 3 month increments – is always going to result in more risk-taking, and more bad decision making. What we see in our firm, is that some folks at the top, who make the most money, see that the window could close on them almost any time, so everything that they do is based on protecting their own personal, financial position. They put all these folks who are familiar to them on to the board, and do everything possible that they can to make the most possible money that they can, as quickly as they can. It is incredibly short-term thinking. It's saying, 'here are our numbers this quarter, I don't know how we are going to make them, so were going to take this big risk, we're going to do crazy things, we're probably going to have to commit a little fraud on the books' à la Enron.

And for the smaller frauds, you will see people stealing twenty thousand dollars, and they say 'I'll catch up here, and here' but they never do.

Look at the Wells Fargo case in the media the past 12 months. You had literally hundreds if not thousands of employees actively engaged in fraud. To keep their jobs they had to make those sales goals. So there is a tremendous pressure in some organizations and the internal controls designed to prevent all this are just not sufficient.

Sadly, I don't think that compliance, and setting a 'tone from the top', is as important as it needs to be in finance. Compliance in investment banking is, I think, viewed often as an unpleasant obligation, like getting your tyres replaced on your car when you don't really feel like going to the garage.

Some financial institutions could care less about compliance – because it doesn't make them money. You can pretty much do what you like if you are making your numbers – nobody cares.

Q. *Do you think that employees can be pressured by an unethical culture to be unethical – or is an honest employee always going to remain honest?*

I think that organisations have personalities, and cultures. I think that a corrupt organisation that allows or condones unethical behaviour – or is at least indifferent to it – will co-opt a lot of employees into engaging in corrupt behaviour. Going back to the Wells Fargo example, I don't think those hundreds or thousands of employees who created phony accounts would necessarily have acted unethically in a different environment. I think that's pretty clear.

Going back to our evolutionary need or desire to conform socially. There is a strong need for complete conformity in larger organisations. So if you are working for a major bank, it's all about conforming. Consequently, some people who rise to the top don't have the most integrity, necessarily, or the most skills, but are instead the person who just tends to be the most conforming. There are companies where the CEO sets a tone of 'we are going to do whatever we need to do to make our goals. And if that means you commit fraud, and have no integrity, then that's fine, too'.

At Wells Fargo, some people did report misconduct – and they were punished and fired and harassed. So the message in those kinds of organisations can be 'conform or be fired and/or if you try to retain your integrity, we will go after you'.

Q. *What advice do you have to employees who feel pressured into acting unethically, or who wish to report a criminal activity but feel too scared to do so, in case they are fired?*

First of all, I think the bravest kinds of people I've ever seen are those whistleblowers who, knowing full well they are likely to suffer, are still willing to report, either internally or externally, to the SEC or SFO. They're the bravest people in the world.

I've seen first-hand how damaging that process is to the individual. I was retained in a whistleblower case about a year ago and I was asked to assist the whistleblower, who had reported a massive fraud that he had been fully a part of. He then decided 'I just can't do this anymore'. He reported his crimes to the FBI and was harassed by the people he worked for. His life fell apart. He ended up with multiple criminal charges of intoxication, lost his second job, his family left him for a period of time . . . he basically broke down.

It's a very hard thing to do, to report fraud to the authorities. Most people can't do it. So if you are going to do it, recognise first off that it's one of the hardest things you can do and understand what the consequences are. Be prepared to lose your job. Be prepared that your friends – your co-workers – might not like you anymore. But know that you are doing the right thing. It takes a lot of integrity and guts.

One thing you can do – there are a lot of great legal firms and organisations that support whistleblowers financially, who are really savvy, who understand the risks.

Special feature: breaking news

*Jack Rees is a former associate producer for morning and even-
ing news shows across a major American TV Network. Previously
a media communications trainer for NATO and TV news writer for
Australia's biggest morning network news show, Jack consults as
a Rights and Clearances specialist in media law and licencing for
TV Networks and online news platforms.*

Q. What role do you think the media plays in exacerbating market
    up- and downswings?

Traditionally, the mainstream media was the sole fount of reporting on the vagaries of capitalist market systems and processes
and was where most people, including traders, looked for perspective, commentary or quasi-soothsaying of what the future held.

Now, of course, there is a plethora of media voices, a cacophony
of social media – Twitter, Facebook and so forth – that can be
cherry picked, manipulated, and so on – leaving us back in the
great age of the English pamphleteers during the printing press
explosion of the 1600s, where a chorus of opinions and naysaying
was made possible, and where opinion and rumour masqueraded
as 'news'.

That said, the average day trader is cut of a certain cloth, and
their disposition leads one to conclude that their perspective on
the market might often be a narrow one. The media knows this;
day traders are, by and large, working in small time increments.
What the media understands is that these traders have high stakes
and are jittery – in part because of their limited margins of error,
their limited perspective and the fact that they are, after all, there
to make a buck – not to provide long-term financial stability. It is
the very human nature of capitalist reward systems that makes the
upswings and depressions or recessions inevitable. In order to get
these traders motivated, capitalism requires risk (enterprise and
speculation) and reward.

In conclusion, the media knows that the traders are fickle, jittery
and in it for the money – and that they adopt a short-term position –
and that is why the media reports the way it does.

Capitalism, as a vehicle for human motivation towards enterprise, has never proved a stable system – take for example the Dutch credit crunch of the mid-1700s. The knock-on effect was redundancies in the American colonies and not long after, revolution in 1776 against British taxation demands. The long and the short of it, as Shakespeare put it, is that 'Man is a giddy thing'.

Q. Would you say that the recent 2016 US presidential election campaign provides a good example of the power of the media in guiding sentiment?

Trump effectively achieved a 1980s-style hostile take-over. And of course, Trump was not a politician. He didn't sound like one, didn't act like one – but he is an EXPERT at performing for the media, in public, and is a star.

Anyone who has seen JFK or Ronald Reagan speak and engage will see a resonance with what Trump has. There's a simplicity in language and there's an appeal to the average American that is very powerful.

Q. How much do you think the modern-day 24/7 financial news cycle affects a trader's ability to trade rationally?

Perhaps traders are embarrassed by the extent to which luck plays a role in their successful trades. It is quite possible that this kind of 'financial porn' provides a way for traders to feel that there is a real faculty of learning and a well of arcane knowledge to be imbibed before, say, dumping stock or buying a million – when in fact luck and gut instincts plays a far more central role.

The vast money and shaky foundations often associated with the vocation have perhaps demanded a romanticism of trading – the greatest example thus far: *Wall Street* (1987) – and it pays some traders and sellers of finance and trading programs to pretend that they are far more technically adept and knowledgeable than they really are.

Ultimately, how cynical should traders and investors be when evaluating news? Media channels exist these days to make money, to sell advertising, and to report on news that the audience is interested in. That is the business of news.

The journalist, however, wishes to expose truth and give a voice to issues – through storytelling or straight reporting. They are not easy bedfellows.

In this age, simply look and listen to the huge choice of news from everywhere – we are spoilt for choice and by reading widely we are best defended against being force fed news like a French Goose on grain.

Notes

1 'greed'. (n.d.). *Oxford Living Dictionaries*, accessed at: https://en.oxforddictionaries.com/definition/greed.

2 Commonly attributed to Einstein, although it may have originated with a different author: ultimately, it has not been proven or disproven to have originated from Einstein.

3 For further reading, the reader is directed to N. K. Logothetis, *What we can and what we can't do with fMRI*, Max Planck Institute for Biological Cybernetics Tübingen, Germany, and Imaging Science and Biomedical Engineering, University of Manchester, Manchester, UK, accessed at: https://mail.google.com/mail/u/0/?tab=wm#search/dian/15b234a8aa8cdac6?projector=1.

4 The first edition was printed in 1871.

5 The *Wall Street Journal* nevertheless reports with exceptional quality on many other matters.

6 A heuristic is a usually speculative formulation that serves as a guide in the investigation or solution of a problem.

3   Trading long or short on stress?

> I liken it to the steroid era in Major League Baseball; it wasn't about right
> and wrong but about getting an edge in a game where the stakes were huge.
> — Turney Duff, former trader, Galleon Group (Lattman, 2013)

According to Turney Duff – a recovering cocaine addict and alcoholic – the
Galleon Group, where he was employed as a stock trader, constituted one
of the most hedonistic organisations in the world. Tales of lavish parties,
prostitutes (actually on the payroll), drugs and insider trading characterised
the heady reminiscences of his time at Galleon. In 2011, however, the party
was over. The music stopped playing as the SEC (Securities and Exchange
Commission) obtained a record financial penalty of $92.8 million against
Raj Rajaratnam, CEO of Galleon, for widespread insider trading. Rajaratnam was also sentenced to a term of imprisonment of 11 years, and was
ordered to pay more than $53.8 million in forfeiture of illicit gains and
$10 million in criminal fines as a result of his crimes. The total amount
of monetary sanctions imposed on Rajaratnam in civil and criminal cases
exceeded $156.6 million. The prolific and enduring existence of fraud in
the financial markets constitutes one of the greatest sources of stress to traders and investors and is a phenomenon that we will investigate in depth
throughout this chapter.

Preet Bharara, United States Attorney for the Southern District of New
York (and recently summarily dismissed by President Trump), was in charge
of Rajaratnam's prosecution. Around that time, Bharara delivered a speech
to NYU law school students, where he spoke of 'epic frauds surfacing with
increasing frequency . . . There is a lack of faith in the economic system;
a lack of belief in the markets; and a lack of trust that the playing field is
level' (Bharara, 2009). Most tellingly he commented: 'When sophisticated
business people begin to adopt the methods of common criminals, we have
no choice but to treat them as such'. These words echo those of Jeff Klink,

the CEO of Klink & Co., who was profiled in Chapter 2's Special feature ('The common denominator in fraud is opportunity') and who spoke of the need to regulate human nature.

Klink's words certainly hold weight. In 2016, for example, JP Morgan Chase & Co agreed to settle SEC charges amounting to $264 million in relation to violations of the Foreign Corrupt Practices Act (FCPA). The bank had hired around 100 interns and full-time employees in well-remunerated roles (at the request of foreign government officials) in order to win approximately $100 million of contracts. As stated by Andrew J. Ceresney, Director of the SEC Enforcement Division,

> JPMorgan engaged in a systematic bribery scheme by hiring children of government officials and other favored referrals who were typically unqualified for the positions on their own merit. JPMorgan employees knew the firm was potentially violating the FCPA yet persisted with the improper hiring program because the business rewards and new deals were deemed too lucrative.

In another recent example, in December 2016, Platinum Partners founder Mark Nordlicht and six other Platinum executives were arrested on multiple charges of securities fraud, wire fraud and investment adviser fraud totalling $1 billion. The fraud was described by US Attorney Robert Capers as 'one of the largest and most brazen investment frauds perpetrated on the investing public' (Lynch, 2016).

Neither case was particularly remarkable in the wider scheme of things. In Q1 of 2017 alone, trading suspensions were issued to NewGen BioPharma Corporation; China Biopharma, Inc., et al.; Ubiquity, Inc.; Desarrolladora Homex; S.A.B. de C.V.; CirTran Corp., et al.; the aforementioned Platinum Pari-Mutuel Holdings Inc.; and PixarBio Corporation. In the same short period, 81 civil lawsuits were brought by the SEC to federal court, with 187 SEC settlements made over the same period. A recent $630 million Deutsche Bank fine for money laundering attests to the fact that some of these violations are stunningly large.

Hedonistic accounts of trader excess remain and will always constitute the stuff of legend. Bernard Madoff, architect of a $60-billion Ponzi scheme, for example (for which he received a 150-year jail sentence), was reportedly such a prolific cocaine user that his office earned the moniker 'The North Pole'. Following an $85 billion post-2008 financial crisis bailout, AIG executives faced investigation for holding a company getaway at a $1000-per-night luxury resort in Arizona. And whilst the markets no longer display the *Barbarians at the Gate*-esque level of hedonism that they once did, fraud still remains an enduring, multi-billion-dollar problem.

A seemingly unwavering public appetite for tales of Wall Street excess (e.g. *Wolf of Wall Street* (2013) – Scorsese's highest income film ever – *Margin Call* (2011), *Wall Street* (1987)) underscores the fact that we all remain as fascinated as we are horrified by these excesses, perhaps betraying a fascination with those extremes of human nature which, given the opportunity, many of us might also share.

It also constitutes a unique source of stress. For whilst traders and investors rely on fundamental data analysis, market excesses, market manipulation and fraud can drive assets in unpredictable ways, severely impacting profits.

Testosterone: the alpha hormone

It has been argued that 'dark' personality traits – e.g. impulsivity or narcissism – are identifiable via one's endocrinology (e.g. Pfattheicher, 2016), with particular attention paid to the 'alpha hormone' – testosterone. Testosterone is a powerful endogenous steroidal hormone that has been hypothesised to play a role in fraud and overly risky behaviour. It has been said, for example, that 'high testosterone investors have a higher craving for monetary risk taking and are more probably to surrender to definite impulsivity-related pathologies' (Stenstrom & Saad, 2011, p. 254).

At first glance, traders and high testosterone seem willing and useful bedfellows, given the fact that high testosterone levels were found to correlate with higher intraday profits (e.g. Coates & Herbert, 2008). But there is a major potential downside. In a study of 4,462 males, for example, Dabbs (2000, p. 82) found that men with high testosterone were more likely to have gotten into trouble at school and with the law as adults, to have used drugs and alcohol, to have been promiscuous and to have gotten a divorce, to violate prison rules, if incarcerated, and to have committed violent crimes. Testosterone contributes to opportunistic behaviour (Lefevre et al., 2013), and high levels of testosterone have been associated with narcissism[1] and dominance (Pfattheicher, 2016), a higher likelihood of cheating and non-reciprocation of trust, and even prejudicial beliefs (Goetz et al., 2013).

The dominant behaviours associated with testosterone can also produce a defensive ego-protective response (Dickerson & Kemeny, 2004). A recent example can be found in Baupost CEO Seth Klarman's recent criticism of the prolific tweeting of President Donald Trump: 'In a job where words matter and nuance matters more, tweeting is not a communication tool, it's pure indulgence' (2016, p. 6). Trump's tweets are often ego-protective and suggest a high need for dominance so classic of a high-testosterone male. This kind of ego-protective response is damaging as it drives the markets further away from rational facts and analysis and closer to emotional, self-interested knee-jerk responses.

Alpha fraudsters and susceptible followers

One kind of particularly profitable fraud is a boiler room 'pump-and-dump' scheme (reminiscent of Jordan Belfort's *Stratton Oakmont*), where inexperienced investors are persuaded to part with large sums to invest in non-existent or worthless shell companies. Brokers need to be charismatic and charming in order to sell the scam, and research tells us that some people can be more vulnerable than others to this kind of manipulation.

Hypnotic susceptibility, for example, has been found to be mediated by frontal inhibition of the brain (Gruzelier, 2006), with MRI scans identifying a massive deactivation of executive function in the brains of believers of Christian healers (Schjoedt et al., 2011) during a healing event. Believers reported increases in trust toward the healer following a service, and the stronger the observed deactivation, the higher they rated the healer after the event (ibid., p. 125). Perhaps it is no surprise that fraudsters have used religious events as conduits for cons; the image of the charismatic but fraudulent pastor asking for donations whilst invoking the Holy Spirit is a fairly recognisable one. In 2015, for example, City Harvest Church founder Kong Hee was found guilty of a $35 million fraud related to misappropriation of church funds (Watts, 2015), whilst in 2016, Virginia pastor Terry Millender and his wife Brenda Millender were found guilty of defrauding their congregation out of more than $1 million, using funds for risky FOREX trades and for the purchase of a $100,000 car and a $1.75 million house (DOJ, 2016). In 2017, pastor Trevor Gross was charged in a Manhattan court of engaging in lies and corruption in the context of an unlawful bitcoin exchange (Raymond, 2017).

Big men, big lies

It is certainly true that more uninformed traders are far more likely to seek 'reassurance from . . . the "big men" who are believed to know how to play the market' (Galbraith, 1954/1988, pp. 169–171). Unfortunately, these 'big men' are more likely to be charismatic narcissists; Harman notes that 'a lot of traders are narcissistic risk-takers, but they are not all rogue traders' (cited in Winters, 2013, p. 24). Indeed, finance offers 'greater narcissistic possibilities than other management functions' (Schwartz, 1991, p. 262) and 'anyone who hopes to rise to the top of an organisation should have a solid dose of narcissism' (Kets de Vries, 2004, p. 188).

A tendency for investors to follow these charismatic figures injects a great deal of unpredictability into the market, particularly as these figures are often engaging in overly risky strategies, or may have engaged in fraudulent acts, yet operate under the auspices of having generated profits through their superior knowledge of trading. This leads to a situation where the 'more adventuresome financing of investment pays off to the leaders, and others [often ill-advisedly] follow' (Minsky, 1975, p. 126), and consequently, the action of 'a large number of ignorant individuals is likely to change violently as the result of a sudden fluctuation of opinion about factors that are of little importance to long-run yields' (Keynes, 1936b, p. 154). It is this exact behaviour that drives sentiment and contributes to boom-and-bust scenarios.

Given that 'attentional processing and executive function recruit the same frontal regions and therefore compete for resources in critical situations' (Schjoedt et al., 2011, p. 119; also see Egner & Raz, 2007 and Richerson et al., 2003), one is able to see how the seductive lure of a charismatic, handsome broker might be just too enjoyable, and too powerful, for some to reject. Fundamental data analysis – a far more sober companion in this scenario – would subsequently lose the fight for attentional processing, with potentially devastating results.

Testosterone: the face of fraud?

Specifically referring to the role of testosterone in overly risky decision-making, neuroscientist Coates (2012d) notes that banks tend to remove older males from risk-taking roles, and remain male dominated. Both could be a mistake; older males have less testosterone, which might positively affect overly risky behaviours, and females have lower testosterone, which may lower their exposure to excessive risk.[2] Males are prone to more deleterious sensation-seeking than females (Grinblatt & Keloharju, 2009a), largely as a result of differences in testosterone levels; this perhaps explains male traders' propensity for, say, trading higher volumes more over-confidently than his female counterpart (Barber & Odean, 2001).

In a study of facial metrics in US presidential success, for example, men with a high facial width-to-height ratio were cited as being more likely to 'experience a greater sense of power . . . more likely to deceive or cheat when this would increase their financial gain. . . . [and] were more prone to exploit the trust of others'. They are also less likely to exhibit 'poise and polish' (Lewis et al., 2012, p. 855), with the link between facial markers, testosterone and aggression thought to be a 'situationally-contingent manifestation of a broader motivation to achieve status' (ibid., p. 857).

As stated by (Jia et al., 2014, p. 1227), 'we conclude that the facial width-to-height ratio measures a distinct managerial trait', which reflects a really compelling idea: face shape might give an indication of how good a manager might be.

Facial metrics, as it turns out, tell us a fascinating story. They not only give us a measure of testosterone levels (Lefevre et al., 2013), but also, to some extent – incredibly – can predict financial fraud (e.g. Wong et al., 2011). In fact, financial misreporting has been found to be up to 98% higher for CEOs whose faces demonstrate an above-average width-to-height ratio (a marker of high testosterone).[3] This includes a greater likelihood of CEOs and CFOs being cited and accused, by name, in SEC Accounting and Auditing Enforcement Releases. As stated in recently published research:

> A CEO's facial masculinity predicts his firm's likelihood of being subject to an SEC enforcement action . . . an executive's facial masculinity is associated with the likelihood of the SEC naming him as a perpetrator. . . . facial masculinity also predicts the incidence of insider trading and option backdating.
>
> (Jia et al., 2014, pp. 1195–1196)

And they sound different, too: individuals are more likely to recognise males as leaders if they have deeper voices (Dabbs & Mallinger, 1999). Interestingly, observed correlations between CEO performance and facial width-to-height ratio found that the relationship was strengthened when the firms' leadership team was lowest in cognitive complexity (Wong et al., 2011). This suggests that some high-testosterone CEOs, perhaps those with less ethical motivations, are more likely to surround themselves with acolytes and/or individuals who do not possess the intellectual strength or knowledge to adequately challenge or question their decisions. The case of Dick Fuld, former Lehman Brothers CEO, exhibited similar behaviour when he hired CFO Erin Callan. Although Callan might have constituted a stand-out hire for other senior roles, her fundamental lack of accounting expertise would have given him great latitude to continue to misrepresent the company's financial records without being adequately questioned (Zehndorfer, 2015).

The warrior gene

It seems that some traders are more genetically predisposed to take on risk – not only as a result of endogenous testosterone levels, but also as a result of something colloquially referred to as 'the warrior gene'. Traders and investors who carry the MAOA-H gene, for example, are more likely to take on financial risk and are able to make better risk-based decisions (Frydman et al., 2011). Conversely, carriers of the MAOA-L version of the gene are more likely to be aggressive and impulsive, and to choose riskier options. Could this genetic variant predispose some traders to greater vulnerability to commit fraud?

MAOA is a fundamentally important enzyme in the risk-taking process, as it regulates the catabolism of serotonin, dopamine, norepinephrine and epinephrine (Frydman et al., 2011, p. 1). Perhaps unsurprisingly, it is closely related to the pathology of gambling, with carriers of a variant of the MAOA gene – the 7-repeat allele – most likely to seek out novelty and be more exposed to the likelihood of becoming a pathological gambler. What is really interesting here is that both MAOA-L and MAOA-H gene carriers are more likely to take on risk, but those who also have higher level of norepinephrine are more likely to seek an immediate reward. Similarly, traders and investors with a short serotonin allele (5-HT), alongside a 7-repeat version of the dopamine (DRD4) gene, seem to require more dopamine to experience a similar sensation of reward than carriers of other DRD4 repeats and/or long 5-HT (serotonin) alleles. Knowledge of a trader's genetic MAOA gene variant, serotonin allele and dopamine gene version might thus give us a very interesting picture of that trader's capacity to effectively pursue risk and resist short-term rewards, which could carry interesting implications for profit. It could also assist us in minimising potential stressors for traders, as it would allow us to identify whether they might be particularly vulnerable to market sentiment, addictions or the lure of opportunistic trading as a means of realising short-term rewards.

Nature or nurture?

Seth Klarman, CEO of Baupost, recently promised his investors that Baupost will 'remain cautious and disciplined; we will do our utmost to separate reason from emotion, relying on the former while striving to recognize the latter and hold it at bay' (Klarman, 2017, p. 8).

What separates a vastly-profitable investor like Seth Klarman from so many less profitable investors? The answer lies in his ability to reject rhetoric in favour of cold, hard data analysis and avoid the subsequent pitfalls so often associated with over-confident trading. In a recent letter to investors, Klarman noted that

> Wall Street is a place where highly confident people go to work. Unfortunately, overconfidence makes it hard for many to hold on to the possibility that they might be wrong, with potentially painful consequences.

At Baupost we practice humility and moderation, aware of how much we don't and can't know.

—Seth Klarman (2017, p. 10)

As the reader will now know, testosterone plays a significant role in confidence, as it mediates how willing a trader or investor will be in taking on risk. But, as it turns out, testosterone is not the only key protagonist in this story.

The dangers of dopamine

Dopamine exerts a significant effect on an individual's attitude to risk and on their emotional state (Sapra et al., 2012). Adolescents with fewer dopamine receptors make riskier decisions (Steinberg, 2010), and dopamine generally exerts a profound effect on financial decision-making behaviour (Knutson & Bossearts, 2007). The length of dopamine alleles (a genetic variant of dopamine that different individuals are born with) negatively affects dopamine receptor 4 (DRD4) activity, with a decrease in DRD4 activity closely associated with 'novelty seeking, attention deficit hyperactivity disorder, and substance abuse' (Sapra et al., 2012, p. 2).

Traders with high DRD4 levels are less likely to trade in volatile markets, and dopamine levels, as a whole, may be able to assist in predicting one's success as a trader: 'two genetic alleles that affect DA [dopamine] are associated with success at trading stocks on Wall Street' (Sapra et al., 2012, p. 5). Given that the presence of specific alleles in a trader's genetic makeup will strongly influence their trading behaviour (Dreber et al., 2009), dopamine represents an interesting contributory factor in how profitable a trader might subsequently become, and in how he experiences and deals with the stress associated with trading.

IQ, another (at least partially) genetic determinant, also appears to mediate and affect stock market participation (Grinblatt, 2009). Overall, genetics offer a really compelling insight into the factors at play in determining trading behaviour: 'The magnitude of such a genetic factor is very large compared to other individual characteristics . . . an individual's genetic composition is an important determinant of the individual's investment behaviour' (Barnea et al., 2010, p. 30).

Hardwired for success?

Higher-earning traders demonstrate higher activity in the right-anterior insula (an area of the brain activated by financial risk, and which causes feelings of 'pain, anxiety, and disgust'; Smith et al., 2014, p. 10506) than less successful traders. Conversely, traders who traded in a more aggressive way as a result of NAcc (nucleus accumbens) signals performed worse, with higher NAcc activity associated with a greater likelihood of a crash and lower future trading returns, prompting the development of a neuro-behavioural metric to measure the cost of irrational, emotional investing (ibid.).

Known unknowns

How far do genetics determine our exposure to market sentiment? Earlier discussions centring around susceptibility to hypnotism do betray a genetic determinant, but it is still difficult to ascertain how far genetics – or sociali-sation – dictate our responses to market upswings and downswings, to herd-ing and to the simple and enjoyable indulgence of greed. In the midst of a boom, when everyone seems to be getting rich, it is difficult not to join in the hype. For a swathe of (particularly retail) traders and investors who have no real trading knowledge, however, following the herd can lead to tumultuous, poorly thought out and ultimately vastly unprofitable trading decisions. Take the period prior to the 2016 US presidential election, for example, where:

> As of mid-August [2016], $13.4trillion of debt worldwide (largely sovereign) traded at negative interest rates, a mystifying and unprec-edented circumstance in which bondholders willingly obligate them-selves to pay interest to issuers for the privilege of tying up their capital for a significant interval while still bearing the risk of default . . . these top of the market bond offerings pose numerous risks that investors seemed to be ignoring.
>
> (Klarman, 2017, p. 1)

This observation was written by Seth Klarman, Baupost CEO, and what he is alluding to is the fact that market hubris, not rational analysis, led to really confusing trading outcomes. In particular, a lot of Main Street investors invest in the words of trading 'gurus' who have historically made profitable trades, or at least have claimed to.

> You sometimes hear a belief on Wall Street that losing a lot of money is a badge of honor and a proof of competence. It means you were good enough that someone trusted you with that much money, and confident enough to take a lot of risk with that money. Sure you lost it, but what are the odds of that happening twice?
>
> (Levine, 2016)

Turns out the odds of that happening are pretty high. Brain scans of traders (Smith et al., 2014) indicate that traders who respond more aggressively (i.e. placing more trades, for greater amounts) as a result of nucleus accumbens (NAcc) signals earn less, again indicating a genetic component. In this way, neural activity could arguably be used as a biomarker for trading behaviours – particularly during market bubbles (Smith et al., 2014). The researchers stated further that 'when the . . . NAcc moving average is high, the empirical probability of a crash is more than four times greater' (ibid., p. 10504).

Early warning systems

Interestingly, a subset of traders in the study were found to possess some kind of early warning signal in the insular cortex region of their brain, which enabled them to make the decision to sell before a stock had reached its highest price and thus exit the market before a crash: 'Lower levels of NAcc activity are associated with higher future returns and low likelihood of a crash, whereas higher levels of NAcc activity are associated with low future returns and increased likelihood of a crash' (Smith et al., 2014, p. 10506).

We are more likely to see sentiment-driven investing amongst retail investors, attributable in part to a lack of technical/financial education in their view of trading as a form of sensation-seeking and entertainment. Nowhere is this more emergent than in the rapidly growing ETF sector.

The (often) uninformed retail investor: exploding ETFs

Launched in November 2014, the multi-award-winning PureFund ISE Cyber Security ETF (Symbol: HACK) managed to raise a still-historic $1.4 billion in only eight months, perhaps one of the most spectacular rises of any ETF in history. The catalyst? A wholly coincidental – and globally reported – hacking of Sony Pictures Entertainment only 12 days after HACK's launch (Burger, 2017). It was a cyber hack that formed the backbone of a juicy, salacious story of backbiting and bitching amongst Hollywood's finest – a story that found the front pages of every media outlet from the *New York Times* to *Vanity Fair*, covering Bloomberg, the *Financial Times* and a multitude of cable TV shows in-between. It moved the issue of cyber hacking immediately to the forefront of public consciousness, with the HACK ETF gaining unbelievable exposure and interest as a result.

PureFund CEO Andrew Chanin capitalised hugely on this opportunity, using charismatic and appealing references to the HACK ETF as an 'ETF for the people' (Anon., 2016). Another example was his claim that 'you can almost say they've democratized investing. The little guy is accessing the very same markets – for the same cost – as the big guys' (Balchunas, 2016). This might be true, but as the reader will learn, human nature seems to get in the way of these exact benefits.

Fast-forward to December, 2015, a few months after HACK's meteoric rise, and ETF trading as a sector had reached historic levels, including a $4.3 billion record trading volume of the two biggest junk bond ETFs in the world – BlackRock's HYG junk bond ETF (in this instance, made up mostly of smaller trades – mostly <$10 million) and State Street's JNK. It was a rise that prompted legendary investor Carl Icahn to predict 'a meltdown in high-yield that will be exacerbated by ETFs' (Rennison & Foley, 2015). Howard Marks, co-founder of Oaktree Capital Management, was similarly moved to call out BlackRock as a 'very dangerous company' because of their extensive activity in the junk bond space. Yet it has only caused significant concern to form amongst more established institutional investors.

The SEC is currently moving toward tighter regulation, particularly of leveraged ETFs, in a space that has escalated rapidly to around $20 trillion traded in ETFs in 2016 and which represents around 25% of daily trading volume; FINRA (the Financial Industry Regulatory Authority) and IMF (International Monetary Fund) have subsequently issued warnings of their threat to global financial security, with BlackRock CEO Larry Fink voicing concern that leveraged ETFs 'could blow up the whole industry' (Loomis, 2014). Bloomberg have referred to the growth in ETFs as a 'passive revolution' (Balchunas, 2017), reflecting comments – and pecuniary warnings – that

> Passive investors are effectively piggy-backing on the most efficient, optimal, market portfolio. However, if the asset base becomes too large, passive investing may prevent market efficiency and lead to a misallocation of capital.
>
> (Kolanovic & Kaplan, 2017, p. 6)

It remains to be seen whether we might be headed for a '*Jurassic Park*-esque disaster . . . Time will still tell if the doomsday scenario will materialize for bond ETFs' and whether exchange traded funds really are 'eating the US stock market' (Wigglesworth, 2017; Hulbert, 2017). Such assertions, similarly representative of the dangers posed by ETFs, were voiced by both the *Financial Times* and *USA Today* in Q4 2016/Q1 2017, with legendary investor Carl Icahn noting that

> in the market today, the danger is that you have all this money pouring in America into ETFs, and ETFs are sort-of almost blind buying. You just buy these ETFs and I always question the fact that if you're buying

these stocks and you really don't know what you own, you're prone to these periods of time – there could be some kind of crisis and there could be a problem.

(Isbitts, 2017)

Similarly, retired CEO and co-founder of Vanguard (today one of the largest US issuers of ETFs) Jack Bogle warned that 'exchange-traded funds are fine just so long as you don't trade them', remarking that some ETFs are sold by 'financial buccaneers' and that investors must avoid the 'lunatic fringe of ETFs' (Damato, 2016).

From active to passive

ETFs and index-tracking – passive investing strategies – have indeed witnessed an explosion in growth, with global inflows averaging over $12,000 per second in 2016. The growth has been particularly rampant in the US given taxation and cost-related benefits – it remains easier to structure cheap ETFs than to accurately track the market. ETFs now represent approximately 30% of all US trading by value, having risen 17% since the preceding year, with a 50% rise in the year before that (according to Credit Suisse; Vlastelica, 2017). Seven of the ten most actively traded securities on US stock markets in 2016 were ETFs, including the SPY ETF (a $221 billion behemoth of an ETF that tracks the S&P 500). It represents an amazing acceleration toward passive strategies – there are now around 6,600 ETFs listed globally, representing total assets of $4 trillion – and that number is rising fast (Lord, 2017). The fact that cost remains a key driver in the utilisation of ETFs over active strategies remains a boon to the ETF industry, as does the current muted returns of the markets, as overall, net returns are increasingly impacted by cost. The SEC continue to retain a sharp focus on the ETF sector.

But here is the *really* interesting thing: whilst ETFs represent an incredibly popular investment market, in a 5 year analysis of 8,000 clients (Bhattacharya et al., 2017) – and supported by outcomes of the Hulbert Financial Digests' investment tracking study – it was found that passive ETF-inclusive portfolios underperformed the wider market by 2.8%; investors were found to generally perform worse as soon as investing in ETFs occurred, with this decline in value being attributed to the introduction of the ETF into their trading strategy.

ETFs vs. human nature

'We find that individuals investing in passive exchange-traded funds (ETFs) do not improve their portfolio performance, even before transaction costs' (Bhattacharya et al., 2017, p. 1217) – a finding attributed to poor ETF selection and poor market timing, and the fact that utilisation of ETFs generally makes it easier to engage with self-destructive, irrational and emotional investing behaviours (for example, short-term thinking).

When we look at the case study of passive ETF investors, we can see that markets can become very sentiment-driven when investors do not actually understand how to interpret financial and economic data correctly: 'We say that a sentence is factually significant to any given person, if and only if, he knows how to verify the proposition which it purports to express' (Ayer, 1946, p. 48). In other words, there is no point in using financial and economic data if one does not have the technical ability to effectively analyse it. It is now a relatively common realisation that a little knowledge can become a dangerous thing (particularly, perhaps, where money is involved): 'those with limited knowledge in a domain suffer a dual burden: Not only do they reach mistaken conclusions and make regrettable errors, but their incompetence robs them of the ability to realize it' (Kruger & Dunning, 1999, p. 1121).

Aside from a generalised lack of trading and investing expertise, there are other trends in passive retail investing that can contribute to market fragility. Bhattacharya et al. (2017), for example, reported that ETF investors tended to be slightly younger and wealthier but lost on average 1.6% per annum as a result of ETF investment. Of this differential, 0.77% was attributable to poor timing with ETF selection not statistically significant. These investors also tended to have a shorter relationship with their bank, a higher exposure to risky securities and a tendency to over-trade, suggesting a motivation, or proclivity for sensation seeking, entertainment or gambling-related trading over the singular pursuit of profit.

Compared to more traditional buy-and-hold strategies, ETF investors underperformed by 1.69% annually, exhibiting overconfidence and over-trading; 'though investors who trade more have worse ETF timing, no groups of investors benefit by using ETFs (Bhattacharya et al., 2017, p. 1217) How to reverse this trend for losses? Take a longer-term strategy and avoid over-trading. Bhattacharya and colleagues (2017, p. 25) noted:

> Our counterfactual analysis thus reveals that if investors would adhere to prescriptions of the literature on how to use ETFs, i.e. track a broad market and use a buy-and-hold strategy instead of abusing them by actively trading, the performance of the ETF part would ceteris paribus increase by roughly 2% per annum.

Unfortunately, the ETF sector encourages emotionality: 'the addition of ETFs makes the full portfolio less efficient' (Bhattacharya et al., 2017) but, as stated by Todd Rosenbluth, Director of ETF and Mutual Fund Research at CFRA, 'unfortunately, the temptation to trade seems to overwhelm many investors' (Waggoner, 2016). The mistakes appear to be overwhelmingly applicable to individual investors, with Bhattacharya and colleagues (2017) concluding that losses are not incurred as a result of choosing the wrong ETFs but as a result of selling the ETFs at the wrong time: 'adopting a buy-and-hold strategy is more important than selecting better ETFs for individual investors'. It clearly warns of the dangers of investing in passive strategies on a short-term basis and provides yet another example of how, when it comes to *nature vs. the markets*, investors do not emerge as the victor.

A pressure to conform

Recalling the words of fraud specialist CEO Jeff Klink in Chapter 2, large financial institutions require conformance – and that can be dangerous.

The data certainly holds up. A 2015 University of Notre Dame study of 1,200 UK and US finance professionals (University of Notre Dame & Labaton Sucharow LLP, 2015) reported that 47% of financial markets professionals thought that competitors had likely engaged in either unethical or illegal activities in order to gain an edge (a statistic that rose to 51% amongst survey respondents earning over $500,000 annually). 37% reported witnessing or gaining first-hand knowledge of wrong-doings in the workplace, with 23% reporting that it was likely that their own colleagues had engaged in unethical or illegal behaviour. A quarter of those surveyed admitted that they would engage in the use of non-public information (i.e. insider trading) for a guaranteed $10 million, if there was a guarantee that they would not be caught – a figure twice as high for younger, less experienced respondents.

Higher earners . . . higher pressure?

Almost 20% of respondents stated that they must at least sometimes engage in unethical or illegal activity in order to be successful (a worry for regulators). Thirty-two per cent said that remuneration structures (e.g. bonuses) might encourage employees to compromise ethical standards or break the law. Individuals earning over $500,000 annually faced further pressures; for example, the same report noted that 27% of survey respondents earning at least $500,000 were subject to company regulations prohibiting them from reporting illegal or unethical practices directly to law enforcement or government agencies. Thirty-nine per cent of all respondents surveyed felt that law enforcement and regulatory agencies were ineffectual in dealing with securities violations (rising to 46% amongst those earning at least $500,000). As stated by Zehndorfer (2015, p. 9), 'without an aggressive plan to stamp out misconduct, we are simply sitting and waiting for another financial disaster to strike'.

Stunningly, and rather depressingly, The Center for Disease Control and Prevention (CDC) reports that individuals working in roles that could be included in the 'sales representatives for financial and business services' category (e.g. investment adviser, broker, trader, investment banker) are 39% more likely to take their own life (when compared to other professional vocations), with financial markets lawyers particularly at risk (lawyers are 54% more likely than average to commit suicide) (Wieczner, 2014). These statistics are sobering and raise the bar even higher in terms of stressing the need to recognise and manage physiological variables (such as chronic cortisol over-production or the development of addictions).

Perhaps it is not a surprise, given the nature of these statistics, that Wall Street psychologist Alden Cass has said that 'out of all the sections of finance, no position do I know of that's more extreme in terms of the emotional endurance one has to have than investment banking' (Wieczner, 2014).

Stocks and suicides

Forced socialisation into an unethical working environment can hold devastating consequences (e.g. Enron, Wells Fargo). At this juncture, a brief (and recent) case study offers a valuable means of contextualising the phenomenon.

In 2016, Ian Gibbons, an exceptionally talented Cambridge graduate and scientist, committed suicide. His wife blamed Theranos CEO Elizabeth Holmes, whose claims of a one-prick blood test had built her a billion-dollar company and earned her place on the Forbes Rich List with a net worth of $4.5 billion. Gibbons's task had represented a mountainous and ultimately impossible task; to make Holmes's ambitious claims a scientific and technological reality. Facing a wide-ranging SEC investigation for fraud at the time of this book's publication, Theranos continues to trade, and CEO Elizabeth Holmes continues to defend her technology (e.g. via global platforms such as the Fortune Global Forum) (Primack, 2015). Meanwhile, Forbes recently re-valued their estimate of Holmes's net worth from $4.5 billion, which had earned her a place at the top of their Wealthiest American Self-Made Women, to $0. The power of the Theranos brand, the magnetism of a charismatic CEO and the overwhelming popularity of the message proved just too much for Gibbons. The reader will now be aware of the great power of sentiment in driving and corralling emotions, and nowhere was it more evident (and more destructive) that for Ian Gibbons.

More than 10,000 suicides overall were reportedly tied to the most recent global financial crisis that originated in 2008 (Haiken, 2014). Sadly, these statistics include an increased risk of suicide amongst young traders. Recent cases include Sarvshreshth Gupta, a graduate of the University of Pennsylvania and a Goldman Sachs intern who committed suicide as a result of intense workplace stress. Similarly, Thomas J. Hughes was a 29-year-old investment banker at Moelis and Company whose intense pressure working within his role was thought to have contributed to his death.

The tragic tale of 21-year-old Moritz Erdhardt, an intern at Bank of America/Merrill Lynch, is perhaps the most well-known. Erdhardt, an ambitious and talented young man, had noted himself that 'sometimes I had a tendency to be over ambitious, which resulted in severe injuries' (Mansey & Pancevski, 2013). His death was attributed to an epileptic seizure after a period of long hours and very little sleep. Whilst his tragic death was not attributed to overwork, medical professionals acknowledged that fatigue could have played a clear role in such a scenario.

A City intern commented to the *Guardian* newspaper, around the time of Erdhardt's death, that he enjoyed the high-pressure culture of investment banking, but that it was tough: 'On average, I get four hours' sleep about 70% of the time. . . [but] there are also days with eight hours of sleep . . . Work–life balance is bad. We all know this going in' (Kennedy & Agencies, 2013). Physiological theory tells us that cultivating a culture of extremely long hours only serves to ramp up cortisol over-production quicker and exacerbate the high-risk culture of trading; this is then over-amplified by excitation-transfer of emotion in a male-dominated, testosterone-driven trading environment. The sum total of these outcomes is irrational and ultimately unprofitable trading – and, as it also turns out – a high rate of depression and suicide.

Embracing hedonism

Returning to the crazy story of Turney Duff that opened this chapter, is it any wonder that Wall Street is considered one of the most, if not *the* most, hedonistic working culture in the world? Consider, for example, Turney Duff's advice to Goldman Sachs Class of Summer MBA programs, to whom he was invited to speak. One of the interns asked Duff after his speech, 'If I'm your broker and I want to increase my business with your hedge fund, what's the best thing for me to do?' Duff's answer? 'You can start by taking me to Vegas' (Lattman, 2013).

In a sobering nod to the gambling and addiction excesses discussed in previous pages, the *New York Times* reported thus: 'If Mr. Duff partied his way to the top, he snorted his way to the bottom. When cocaine enters the picture, Mr. Duff's Wall Street confessional becomes an addiction memoir' (Lattman, 2013). Perhaps cocaine also played a key role in the fall of Bernie Madoff, if the reader recalls the 'North Pole' comments, and perhaps it remains – alongside other addictions – a defining force in the emergence of irrational and emotional investing.

Whilst the *Barbarians at the Gate*-esque excesses of the 1980s and 1990s seem to be somewhat behind us, it nevertheless remains a fact that the markets are a hedonistic place. And it is perhaps true that our resistance to these kinds of excesses (e.g. fraud, addiction) is weakened by a failure of orthodox economic theory to analyse, or even recognise, them.

Weakened resistance

The principle of hedonism recognises the fact that 'pleasure and pain are as much the province of logic as are harmony and discord' (Gassendi, 1972, p. 360). It seems clear, therefore, that developing a strategy to analyse emotions – as motivations to trade – would greatly strengthen the efficacy of a trade or position alongside the use of financial and economic data analysis. Conversely, a failure to understand or recognise the power of emotion might end in very unprofitable or unwise trade execution.

Unfortunately, many traders have what might be considered a weakened resistance to market sentiment, simply because orthodox economics theory tells them that it is not important. And this represents a unique source of stress, as it makes them far less able to predict market movements.

How might hedonism, a concept that shaped economic thought as far back as Ancient Greece, have become suddenly so irrelevant? Proponents of orthodox economics theory contend, for example, that 'value judgements have no theoretical sense. Therefore, we assign them to the realm of metaphysics' (Carnap, 1981, p. 150).

This phenomenon can, in fact, be traced to the 1930s, where a desire for theory unification by the dominant philosopher/scientists of the time (logical positivists) led to the expulsion of hedonism, and the role of emotion in general, from economic theory. The metaphysical stance of logical positivism was that reality consists only of what is directly observable, and that the goal of science was to generate predictable, generalizable, robust outcomes utilising the scientific method. Whilst this approach has contributed incredibly to advancements in the natural sciences, it nevertheless appears far more problematic to traders and investors who also need to factor in a lot of ungeneralizable, unseen yet highly powerful factors (e.g. a culture of fraud, greed, panic) to their analyses of each trade.

What remains interesting is that some of the most successful traders do just that. Take Howard Marks, the CEO of Oaktree Capital, a fund with $100 billion AUM (Assets Under Management). Marks can be considered an extremely successful investor, having achieved a net worth of $1.89 billion. Marks rejects the orthodoxy of relying exclusively on traditional analysis, as is the prevalent practice in orthodox economics theory, instead valuing '*deep thinking*';

'Given the near-infinite number of factors that influence the future, the great deal of randomness present, and the weakness of the linkages, it is my solid belief that future events cannot be predicted with any consistency . . . with anything approaching the accuracy required for them to be helpful.' Marks recognises the need to integrate all kinds of analyses – not only traditional analysis, but analyses of social and human factors (often not predictable) – when placing a successful trade. Similarly, George Soros, one of the most successful investors in history, with a personal net worth of around $25 billion, reaches a similar conclusion, that 'economic reality is actively shaped by the perceptions of market participants' (Cymbalista, 2003, p. 1). Soros recognises that understanding emotions and social factors remains critical in executing effective trading strategies.

Currently, a small coterie of specialist research companies (e.g. ESG Ratings, previously known as GMI Ratings) also recommend utilising such an approach. ESG Ratings, for example, produces an annual 'Black Swan Risk List' which has, in the past, proved prescient. The AGR (Accounting, Governance and Regulatory) model developed by GMI Ratings that underpins the Black Swan List provides a useful barometer of 16 measures of risk that 'most commonly represent . . . stocks before the precipitous loss of shareholder wealth' (GMI Ratings, 2013). These measures consider a range of factors pertaining to human, social and cultural factors in their analyses, alongside the use of more traditional financial data analysis.

'I have to race the race'

Luckily, the barometer is shifting in favour of a recognition of the key role of emotions in trading and investing, and in recognising that orthodox approaches (whilst effective in many ways) really do have their limitations:

Machines will not do well in assessing regime changes (market turning points), forecasting trends over longer time horizons, and situations which involve interpreting human behaviour (e.g. politicians, central bankers, investors' fear and greed, etc.).

(Kolanovic & Kaplan, 2017, p. 7)

This is echoed by the sentiment that 'identifying bubbles and predicting crashes from price data alone is a notoriously difficult problem' (Smith et al., 2014, p. 10503), and that the time has now come to build physiological and other data into our observations in order that the most effective and profitable trading and investing strategies can be executed.

Ultimately, in the words of Olympic athlete Mark deJonge: 'Predictions are predictions. If you could predict the stock market, you would be super rich'. deJonge goes on: 'But I have to race the race. It doesn't matter what I've done over the last few years. I have to race at the Olympics' (Hall, 2016). What deJonge tells us here is that economic predictions are just that, predictions – and in the reality of that split-second moment when a trade (or a medal-winning performance) is executed, reality gets in the way; and we must know how to manage it. Ultimately, if traders and investors want to strengthen their resistance against the power of market sentiment, then the first step they need to take is to fully recognise it. And that might lead to less stress and greater profits.

Addicted to stress

Many people are not aware that it is possible to become addicted to stress. Whilst stress can, in the short-term, be a positive motivator to action (e.g. innervating and challenging), a stress addiction carries real and dangerous consequences. What is most concerning for traders and investors is that heightened levels of stress increase one's vulnerability to addiction. Addictive behaviour, in turn, can cause impulsive and damaging behaviours. As stated by Sinha (2008, p. 105):

Psychosocial and behavioral scientists have elegantly shown that with increasing levels of emotional and physiological stress or negative affect, there is a decrease in behavioral control and increases in impulsivity, and with increasing levels of distress, and chronicity of stress, greater the risk of maladaptive behaviors.

It is immediately possible to see how damaging these outcomes could be for an investment bank that has a trading floor full of highly stressed traders – particularly in the context of say, the 2007 housing bubble and the ensuing 2008 financial crisis. Sinha (2008, p. 105) continues: 'High emotional stress is associated with loss of control over impulses and an inability to inhibit inappropriate behaviors and to delay gratification'. Business is set up for quarterly reporting and sometimes daily, if not hourly, benchmarking of profits. This is exceedingly damaging, as it hugely encourages these inappropriate, impulsive behaviours through valuing short-term profits over all else. The fact that traders who make huge losses (as well as huge gains) can still command huge bonuses is testament to how ingrained this kind of impulsive thinking has become.

High stress, low control

The way that traders and investors experience this kind of increased impulsivity is as follows; when the brain processes the fact that we are under stress, the part of the brain (prefrontal cortex) that is responsible for impulse control becomes less effective. At the same time, the limbic region (responsible for risk-taking) actually gears up.

> Neurobiological evidence shows that with increasing levels of stress, there is a decrease in prefrontal functioning and increased limbic-striatal level responding, which perpetuates low behavioral and cognitive control. Thus, the motivational brain pathways are key targets of brain stress chemicals and provide an important potential mechanism by which stress affects addiction vulnerability.
>
> (Sinha, 2008, p. 107)

As we can see from the quote above, the net effect of stress is that, in the short-term, traders become neurobiologically less able to 'rein themselves in', which can cause overly risky trading. The net effect in the long-term is that traders and investors can become more vulnerable to addictions – including an addiction to stress.

As stated by Concordia University neuroscientist and addiction specialist Jim Pfaus, 'stressors can also wake up the neural circuitry underlying wanting and craving – just like drugs do' (Schreiber, 2012). High-profile examples of this kind of behaviour can be found in former Pimco (and now Janus Capital Group) bond trader William Gross, who would sometimes wake up three times a night to check his Bloomberg account. Greg Coffey, an ex-trader who regularly turned over his entire $5 billion portfolio three times *daily* is another example. Coffey only stopped this extreme practice after an intervention by his wife, which ultimately led to him deciding to walk away from his trading role (Butcher, 2016).

Workaholics and adrenaline junkies

Professor Judith Orloff, assistant clinical professor at the University of California, explains stress addiction as a behaviour where 'people are tired and they want a rush . . . We become adrenaline junkies, which leads to workaholism' (Nuwer, 2014). Workaholism is really an addiction to work; traders and investors are, as we have seen, exceedingly vulnerable to this condition. Workaholism and stress addictions both contribute to the 'leisure sickness' phenomenon, where traders and investors regularly become sick during downtime (e.g. vacations). This is attributable, in part, to adrenal fatigue, where the trader has become, by this point, dependent on adrenaline to keep going as they are so stressed. This represents a critical sign in knowing that the body has too much to cope with, and it is the point where physiological interventions become necessary. The reader will be happy to hear that these exact interventions are all detailed in Chapter 4.

Trader physiology: key takeaways

- The financial markets are inherently unpredictable. Unpredictability spikes cortisol, the stress hormone, with long term exposure risking adrenal fatigue and burnout;
- Long-term stress exposure can cause death of brain tissue (and therefore lowered IQ) and compromised cognitive function – which is very bad news for traders who rely on intellectual capacity, rapid-fire thinking and the ability to make fast, predictive decisions;
- Traders remain vulnerable to the development of addictions, given the over-stimulating effects of trading on neurotransmitter pathways;
- Finance is a high stress vocation, with some evidence of pressure (particularly amongst high earners and, from a conformity perspective, new/ younger hires) to act unethically, or to engage in excessive short-term thinking to meet the short-term targets of clients and senior management;
- Herding, a quintessentially irrational behaviour, may result in part from a desire amongst traders to stick close to colleagues and competitors, and to not risk 'breaking away' from the herd by making riskier, innovative or unusual trading decisions.

Special feature: hazing – from sports to stocks

The work hard, play hard culture of many financial institutions engages young traders in a hyper-masculinised, competitive, high-testosterone culture, where conformance to social norms is heavily encouraged. I spoke to leading sociologist Dr Natalie Darko, who has worked with and studied male behaviours in elite rugby teams, about the dangers that such a hyper-masculinised environment might pose to young males on both a trading floor and a sports field.

Q. *Do you feel there are similarities between the hazing (initiation rituals) in sports teams for young athletes and the conditions in which young traders enter trading roles?*

Hazing – or what can be defined as initiation testing – was a prominent part of the sports teams I have observed and remains a customized activity across varies levels of university and grass-roots rugby teams. New recruits – or wannabe fresher players who want to join the legendary elite team that I worked intimately with – would seem willing to do anything that the senior players required in order to be part of the team. It's a common phenomenon in heavily socialised male-dominant environments.

This meant that they were immediately willing to engage in the concomitant constructed hegemonic rugby masculinity/ies that this environment required of them, such as excess drinking, drinking pubic hair or pints of mess. For example, the fresher players were given excessive amounts of alcohol to drink, then were then taken on a bus whilst blindfolded. They were then stripped and dumped at a random location. Their test was to run back to the campus as quickly as possible, whilst naked.

I remember that during one initiation, one (naked) athlete distracted a female driver who then crashed into a barrier. This made the local press and the player was reprimanded by the coaching staff for failing to adhere to the professionalism of the elite club.

It is questionable whether the players themselves would classify their rugby initiations as a form of exploitation as categorized within traditional conceptualizations of hazing, because these men were highly willing to partake in the extreme activities because it allowed them to conform to the expected rugby masculinity and concomitant elite status ascribed to these men from other male players, the student cohort on campus, and from others at other universities.

But it arguably forces conformity, which is where the line between ethical and unethical can become compromised extremely quickly.

The constructed hegemonic conditions of a trading floor might carry different elements, e.g. showing they can live through excessive working hours, but the outcome in terms of conformity and socialisation is still most likely the same, and that carries potentially damaging outcomes for the individual and organisation.

In the research I conducted, the players did not actually have space to 'manage out' stress – which is a similar situation that young traders and financiers might well also be facing. They did not feel that they could reveal any form of stress or anxiety with anyone within the club because of the feared ramifications to their professional sporting career and essentially they could not risk being 'dropped' to a lower team.

I would suggest that traders would also experience the same issues and fail to reveal these comparable concerns, and it is an area that would benefit from further study.

Q. Are these socialised hyper-masculine behaviours a result of nature (e.g. high testosterone levels) or nurture (i.e. required conformity)?

My research indicated that performance of the public 'front stage' rugby masculinity restricted all forms of emotional distress or 'weakness' as this was associated with feminine behaviour. This hence explains why the players would use key quotes such as 'get up shut up and stop being a fanny' if a teammate got injured.

These types of comments were made to players who publicly expressed their emotions – such as pain – during minor injuries, or who complained about being unable to perform. So it was definitely a forced socialised requirement to suppress certain emotions.

Essentially **the cause** is the socially constructed form of hegemonic masculinity that has been and is currently assigned to this elite rugby team by **the players themselves**. There were men who did manage to distance themselves from these hazing activities – but only later as they reached senior year and it was made evident by themselves and by the coaches that their physical abilities were of a potential professional class.

They were therefore able to justify their withdrawal on account of signing professional contracts. However, there were only a very small percentage of players who were able to take this route – and all of them took part in the year one initiations for incoming players. Not many players had an excuse to stop.

Q. Do you see any effects in mental or physical performance for young males who operate in such a male-dominated, competitive environment who do not have an outlet for discussing emotions and stress?

The risks in rugby were clearly evident – for some men there was evidence of stress, high levels of alcohol consumption, depression and withdrawal from normal daily activities – e.g. attending lectures. This occurred because when these men were unable to conform to the expected masculinity of being physical adept and strong with high levels of physicality – on and off the pitch – they felt 'less masculine' or emasculated.

My research didn't clinically classify BDD (Body Dysmorphic Disorder) or MDD (Major Depressive Disorder) *per se* but examined comparable forms of behaviour. It became evident to me that some of the men's narratives exhibited comparable behaviours and signs of stress.

What was highly evident [was that] the **inability to perform in sport** and **detachment from the 'inner masculine circle and ascribed masculinity'** was highly distressing for them.

Young traders entering a highly-masculinised, competitive world might also be at risk of the latter.

The dangers of having nowhere to turn can lead to increased risk taking behaviour, such as drug use, increased alcoholism – or even attempted suicide, as was the case with rugby ace Mathieu Bastareaud.

Suicide rates are higher in finance than many other professions with stress a real danger too, so again I see a potential area for comparison there.

Q. Is there anything you would recommend for the HR or management functions of financial institutions in terms of how they could support young traders and investment bankers better?

My recommendations for HR/managers are that they need to deconstruct the evident elite hegemonic masculinity/ies that exists within this environment and share their experiences of emotional distress or even stress.

It needs to be made evident that it is feasible for young traders to express their stress or anxiety to their managers without ramifications to their position. In my research there was one coach who was a former professional player, who was forced to leave sports due to injury. Unlike many other coaches he shared his feelings during his injury and the emotional distress to his players to show them that it was feasible to experience stress and anxiety, and this was really positive for them. Dwayne 'The Rock' Johnson, an epitome of a hyper-masculinised personality, has also garnered a lot of positive attention for sharing his battles with depression.

I'd also strongly suggest any form of relaxation activity that allows traders to take time away from the stressful context is essential.

Q. *Orthodox economics theory does not recognise the role of emotions and instead relies on traditional quantitative financial and economic analyses. Integrating a more sophisticated analysis of emotions and the physiological mechanisms that underpin them seems like it would be very valuable. What are your thoughts on this?*

Your proposed concept is essential – we cannot escape our positioning in our social context and culture. It informs and shapes our everyday behaviour and actions both consciously and unconsciously – therefore it is vital that we start to explore and consider its impact on our rational and irrational behaviour.

I cannot personally see how it would be possible to really gain an in-depth appreciation of the financial markets without taking this into account alongside financial data.

Special feature: lunch isn't for wimps

In this special feature, I spoke to stress expert and New York Times bestselling author Heidi Hanna, who tells us about the dangers that traders and investors face in terms of stress and stress addiction.

Q. Trading can involve 100-hour working weeks. How is this likely to affect Wall Street interns and senior traders/investors?

The research is clear that we experience the negative consequences of stress when we believe that our capacity is less than the demands on our time and energy.

Basic biological elements such as nutrition, physical activity, and sleep are critical for keeping the brain and body in an optimal performance state. Once energy capacity is compromised – as it often is throughout the workday – toxic stress hormones are released to help drive survival activities. Short term this stress response is helpful and adaptive, but on a chronic basis it kills brain cells, hijacks the ability to think clearly, creatively, or collaboratively, and creates internal wear and tear on the body that likely contributes to 75–90% of all health problems.

This stress sickness is more likely to break down an older individual because they're less flexible and resilient due to the natural aging process. However, with age we also tend to have greater perspective of what matters most in life, more emotional intelligence, stronger social support systems, and financial security, which may provide buffers to stress. Young traders may still believe they're too young to crash, will rest when they're older, and push off important social relationships, community involvement, and self-care under false assumptions that they'll do it as soon as things settle down. Which never happens.

Q. Wall Street intern and graduate programmes generally hire the brightest and best. How might a high-achiever personality be more vulnerable to stress and stress addiction?

Research has demonstrated a connection between a Type A personality and greater susceptibility to the negative effects of stress. Considering the impact of mindset and perception on how the body responds to stress, traits like perfectionism can lead to chronic worry that shifts the lens through which one experiences stress. In their perfectionism, Type As also may isolate when things get tough or feel out of control to protect their image of having it all together, which exacerbates the negative effects of stress even more.

Q. In your view, are traders and investors generally at risk of stress addiction and what kind of form do you think this might take?

Absolutely. Traders tend to be very bright, independent, confident, and like to be in control. From my experience, they work hard and play hard. Many of these personality types also come from families with a history of substance abuse or mental illness, making their brains more susceptible to addictive tendencies. Work, performing, getting positive feedback, and even the rush of taking risks are highly addictive to the brain, as these behaviours act on the same chemical cascade that fuels the reward system intended to keep us wanting more. I expect that many traders find themselves drawn to other addictive behaviours such as gambling, drinking, drugs, spending money, and high risk activities to fuel the adrenaline rush they crave, especially when they are feeling out of control in other areas of their life, unwilling to share their concerns with friends and family, or even just feel tired and unable to wind down.

Q. The academic literature surrounding irrational investing draws a lot of commonalities between trading, gambling and addictive personalities. Do you feel that stress addiction might exacerbate an addiction to the dopamine high of trading, or play a part in moving a trader from a trading to a (problem) gambling mindset?

It may seem counterintuitive that we would be hardwired for stress addiction, but when we experience something potentially threatening the brain wants to make sure we remember it. And memories are solidified in the brain with highly addictive chemicals that may lead us to dependence. What's more, we live in a culture that glamorizes busyness and hyper-connectivity, making it seem weak or lazy to take time off. I think it is quite possible that without realizing it, a trader's brain could non-consciously be pulled to risky behaviours in all aspects of life. And that in some cases the confidence that helps them find success could become problematic overconfidence that would keep them from reaching out for guidance or support from a trusted colleague or advisor, leading to an increased risk of mistakes. What's more, when the brain is overwhelmed our ability to think logically, problem solve, or even consider possible consequences is reduced, creating a dangerous cycle of risk-seeking, overconfidence and isolation.

Q.   What are the outcomes of an untreated stress addiction?

If someone is addicted to stress, they begin to rationalize their behaviours making it feel impossible to slow down and practice self-care. It's estimated that chronic stress may be responsible for 75–90% of all medical visits. Unmanaged stress decreases immune functioning, destroys brain cells, and increases system-wide inflammation. When work stress become addictive, it not only impairs cognitive and emotional function, it can destroy relationships. People show up physically when they need to, but are often still thinking about work when with their families and friends, who can feel their disinterest.

Q.   Research indicates that traders may have higher testosterone levels than non-traders. Does high testosterone play a role in exacerbating the dangers, or onset of stress, or stress addiction?

It's certainly a great hypothesis. My guess is that it wouldn't cause stress or stress addiction but it would perhaps fuel the types of behaviours that make one susceptible to it. One correlation I can think of is that the stress response has been shown to be quite different in males versus females, which likely relates back to testosterone and oestrogen levels. The female response has been labelled Tend and Befriend (Taylor, 2000), and seems to drive women to want to reach out and support others, collaborate, and take care of community or group needs. This may lead to a greater tendency for women to get social support during stress, decreasing the negative impact. Although female traders may have higher than average testosterone levels and therefore a more natural fight–flight response similar to their male counterparts.

Q. *Cortisol (in traders) has been shown to be raised more by uncertainty than by a trading loss: given that the financial markets are perpetually unpredictable, how might this impact negatively on burnout, adrenal fatigue, etc.?*

One of the primary determinants of whether stress is helpful or harmful is the perception of control. We seem to handle bad news better than no news at all because we can move forward with some sort of adjustment once we know the situation. Working in an industry that is based on fluctuations and uncertainty would definitely increase the risk of stress-related issues and burnout. Ironically, it might also be part of what drives certain personality types to seek out this industry. That plus the potential upside, knowing that if it wasn't so hard everyone would be doing it. (And I even heard this said at an advisor conference recently). People who see challenges as opportunities have the ability to be more resilient than most. And I believe traders have greater built in resilience. However, that resilience can only last so long before chronic stress still takes a serious toll.

Q. *In terms of stress addiction, what should a spouse or family member look out for? What, generally, are the signs?*

Inability to relax (obviously), hyper-connection to technology, sleep problems, irritability, brain fog, appetite changes, headaches, stomach aches or other physical symptoms, lack of interest in hobbies they used to enjoy, not making time for social connections outside of work.

Q. *Can stress cause physical symptoms, such as George Soros's famous backaches?*

Stress will absolutely cause physical symptoms, and muscle tension in the back, neck or shoulders are one of the most common in addition to headaches and digestive problems. Some of that is based on the inflammatory effect of stress, rapid heart-rate and shallow breathing, and the fact that digestion and immunity are diminished when the stress response is trying to focus all resources on mobilizing for fight or flight. When we experience stress, the brain and body are trying to get us to act. To change our circumstances, either internally or externally. Like an internal GPS, stress is meant to shine a light on the fact that a course correction is needed. Which is why one of the best ways to decrease stress and increase resilience is physical activity and exercise.

Q. *This book, for the first time, focuses on enhancing a trader's physiology as a means to maximising trader performance. As a stress expert in stress addiction, do you feel that a greater engagement with health and fitness would help mitigate stress addiction?*

Absolutely! And it's why I work with so many people in the financial services industry to help them recharge their internal battery through nutrition, fitness, sleep, social connections, relaxation strategies and brain fitness. Once people realize that it's not their fault they're hooked on stress and believe that a life with oscillation is more effective not only for their health and happiness but also for their business performance, they can start to build in strategic shifts that help them optimize the energy of pressure without it turning into pain.

Q. *What needs to change in the trading and investing culture to minimise the threat of stress addiction?*

Build a culture where it's not lazy to rest, where we don't glamorize the torture of hyper-connectivity and busyness, and instead teach young traders that their most important resource is their energy, and that investing in their own energy is critical to success.

Notes

1 Research indicates the existence of two types of narcissism: grandiose and vulnerable. Furthermore, narcissism represents a sliding scale where a small prevalence of narcissism within a person's personality can actually be a positive and beneficial thing.
2 Also see Anon. (2009). Want to reduce risk? Hire women, older men for trading floor. *Securities Industry News*; J. Coates (2012d), *The Hour Between Dog and Wolf: Risk Taking, Gut Feelings, and the Biology of Boom and Bust* (New York: Penguin Press).
3 Reactive as opposed to basal testosterone, however, might be a more accurate indicator of behaviour: Lefevre et al., 2013.

4 Taming animal spirits

> We find strong empirical support in favour of a geomagnetic-storm effect in stock returns . . . Unusually high levels of geomagnetic activity have a negative, statistically and economically significant effect on the following week's stock returns for all US stock market indices.
>
> — Krivelyova & Robotti, (2003, p. 1)

In 2002, former US Secretary of State Donald Rumsfeld (2002) stated that 'there are known knowns . . . There are known unknowns . . . But there are also unknown unknowns'.

Up to this point, the reader has been taken on a journey through a lot of known–unknowns. Before opening the pages of this book, for example, a trader may have known that his physiology plays a role in shaping his trading preferences, but he is unlikely to have known the true extent to which it has historically directed his behaviour.

Yet there are still some enthralling unknown–unknowns that we have not yet covered. To understand the true power of physiology in trading and investing still requires one more observation: that our physiology remains stunningly reactive to the powerful forces of nature that surround us.

Nature vs. the markets

Nature, it turns out, wields an extraordinary influence on emotions and trading. In a study of four stock markets (NASDAQ, S&P500, Amex, NYSE), geomagnetic storms were found to exert a profound effect on human behaviour, with the effect most prominent during the six days following a storm (the 'recovery' phase). Returns during 'normal' days were substantially higher than on 'bad' (six days post-storm period) days. Effects were represented by a strongly significant and negative relationship between stock returns and geomagnetic storm activity, ranging from

-0.84% to -2.1% (S&P500), -1.11% to -2.40% (AMEX), -1.60% to -2.51% (NASDAQ) and -2.1% to -1.76% (NYSE). This could not be accounted for by the SAD effects (the effects of the well-documented seasonal depressive phenomenon known as Seasonal Affective Disorder) exerted on stock returns, as documented by Kamstra, Kramer & Levi (2003, cited in Krivelyova & Robotti, 2003, p. 24): 'Intense geomagnetic storms not only appear to affect people's mood during their recovery phase but also seem to affect US stock returns within a week from hitting the atmosphere' (Krivelyova & Robotti, 2003, p. 19). Interestingly, the effect is most profound for small cap stocks.

Geomagnetic storms have been correlated with enhanced anxiety, sleep disturbances, altered moods and greater incidences of psychiatric admissions (Persinger, 1987, p. 92, cited in Krivelyova & Robotti, 2003, p. 6), the latter attributable to the circadian (natural 24-hr cycle) rhythm of melatonin production and its effect on depression rates.

Such a seemingly far-fetched yet scientifically valid concept – the idea that the weather affects P&L – is not new. In 1899, for example, Dexter (1899) wrote that poor weather consistently produced negative emotional states and higher death rates than good weather. Similarly, Lawrence Smith (1939) discovered a strong inverse relationship between poor September stock market returns and barometric pressure. He deduced that

> conditions which cause equal deviations in rainfall at New York tend to create equivalent changes in mass psychology, and consequently to the level of stock prices. But these stock price changes may be gains and they may be losses, regardless of the sign of the rainfall deviation. It is then the degree of change ± in stock prices and the degree of deviation in stock prices and the degree of deviation ± in rainfall that appear to be directly associated within the several systems of which they are a part.
>
> (1939, p. 102)

Persinger (1987, quoted in Krivelyova & Robotti, 2003, p. 6) noted that geomagnetic storms are divided into three phases: the initial phase (2–8 hours), main phase (12–24 hours) and recovery phase (tens of hours to days afterward). They generally last 2–4 days, with a higher concentration of storm periods during March–April and September–October. 'The response of human beings to a singular intense geomagnetic storm may continue several days after the perturbation [deviation] has ceased' (Krivelyova & Robotti, p. 5): 'the effects of unusually high levels of geomagnetic activity are more pronounced during the recovery phase of the storms' (ibid., p. 7; e.g. Zakharov & Tyrnov, 2001; Halberg et al., 2000; Belisheva et al., 1995).

Circannual hormonal fluctuations

A study of 11,000 males based in the South West of the USA reported that testosterone–oestrogen ratios were at their lowest observed levels during the month of September, particularly in younger males. Older males also demonstrated a significant decline in DHEA (dehydroepiandrosterone) – the hormone that leads to the production of androgens and oestrogens – during this period, with levels peaking in the spring. Similarly, a study of Norwegian males found a sizeable difference in seasonal testosterone, with lowest levels observed in mid- to late autumn, with others identifying similar seasonal variations in testosterone (e.g. Moskovic et al., 2012, Svartberg et al., 2003; Andersson et al., 2003; Ruhayel et al., 2007). Petersen suggests that

> the effect on the human may vary; in one the reaction time may somewhat delay, in another accelerate in the effects. Occasionally, too, individuals may react in contrary fashion as far as some of the physiological mechanisms are involved, but on the whole, the entire population swings in a chemical and physiological rhythm that is identical.
> (quoted in Lawrence Smith, 1939, p. 29)

It is interesting to observe in this context that seasonal variances in returns demonstrate a significant drop in September (see Figure 4.1),

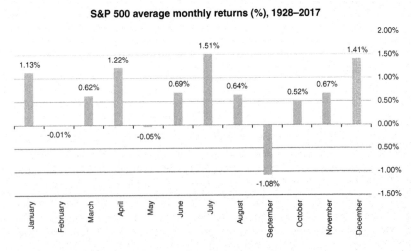

S&P 500 average monthly returns (%), 1928–2017

Figure 4.1 S&P 500 Average Monthly Returns (%), 1926–2017

which *may* suggest a relationship between circannual (annual biological rhythm) variations in testosterone and seasonal variations in P&L returns:

> it is conceivable that circannual variation in sex hormones may be region specific and based on local climate patterns.
>
> (Moskovic et al., 2012, p. 1303)

Loans and lunar cycles

Can a full moon influence P&L? The idea, at first glance, appears even more unlikely than the effect of storms. But the effect of lunar cycles has been observed, specifically in the context of

> strong lunar cycle effects in stock returns. Specifically, returns in the 15 days around new moon dates are about double the returns in the 15 days around full moon dates. This pattern of returns is pervasive; we find it for all major U.S. stock indexes over the last 100 years and for nearly all major stock indexes of 24 other countries over the last 30 years.
>
> (Dichev & Janes, 2001)

The effect is not, interestingly, limited to night-time occurrences; the sun also appears to play a key role, too. Hours of sunshine seem to exert a positive effect on stock returns, too (Hirshleifer & Shumway, 2003), and it has been observed that 'when the magnetic field direction within the solar wind is directed opposite to the earth's magnetic field, then large geomagnetic storms can occur' (p. 5). 'Sunspot activity peaks every 11 years . . . geomagnetic storms correlate with sunspots' (Krivelyova & Robotti, 2003, p. 5). As far back as 1934, an MIT research associate by the name of Harlan Stetson published a scientific report named 'Sun spots and their effects', in which he concluded that

> Variation in radiation, particularly in the ultra violet, is known to be capable of profound biological and physiological changes . . . Buying and selling waves with corresponding fluctuations in commodity prices will, in the long-run, reflect confidence or anxiety on the part of the buying public.
>
> (quoted in Lawrence Smith, 1939, p. 107)

Similar comments can be found in other earlier research studies; for example,

> it is commonly agreed that solar activity has adverse effects first on all enfeebled and ill organisms. In our study we have traced that under

conditions of nervous and emotional stresses (at work, in the street, and in cars) the effect may be larger for healthy people. The effect is most marked during the recovery phase of geomagnetic storms and accompanied by the inhibition of the central nervous system.

(Krivelyova & Robotti, 2003, p. 7)

It can certainly be said, given the weather, lunar and pro-cyclical hormonal data presented here, that, 'like the moth, we are only aware of the more proximal reasons for our behaviour' (Dabbs, 2000, p. 27). Traders and investors need to understand how their physiological design directs their behaviour toward money, other traders, the markets, profit strategies and so on. But – as we have seen here – they also need to appreciate the unseen hand of nature in influencing the strength of their physiological reactions under different scenarios.

They also need to realise one more powerful and important concept. And that is that we can manage and manipulate our own physiology to maximise profitable outcomes.

Trader physiology: key optimisation strategies

The reader has now received a comprehensive introduction to the seminal role of physiology in irrational and emotional trading. It is an introduction that has raised some concerning ideas – a heightened vulnerability to addiction, for example – alongside more positive observations. But there is, of course, one observation left to discuss.

Amazingly, all of the most significant negative concepts discussed in this book (e.g. the death of brain tissue caused by stress) can be completely reversed – and, in fact, optimised – by engagement with exercise and a healthy food intake, alongside other healthy lifestyle adaptations. It subsequently remains a defining goal of this book to empower the reader by engaging him with these adaptive techniques in a way that is pragmatic and instantly applicable.

For ease of reference, these adaptive techniques have been classified into ten 'optimisation strategies':

#1 *Traders and investors: born to run*
#2 *Anabolic arbitrage: lift heavy to trade smart*
#3 *Working out makes you smarter*
#4 *Hedge your exposure to stress and go long on sleep*
#5 *Hungry for success? Eat right to trade and invest better*
#6 *Use music as a performance tool*
#7 *Harness the power of nature*

#8   *We are hardwired to herd*
#9   *Embrace hedonism*
#10   *Willpower is finite; use it wisely*

These 'Ten trader optimisation strategies' will now be discussed individually, with key recommendations for action provided at the conclusion of each one.

#1 Traders and investors: born to run

In the words of the Boss, Bruce Springsteen (1975), 'in the day we sweat it out on the streets of a runaway American dream'. And Wall Street traders are, funnily enough, sweating it out, on the Street, day after day, as they trade. Often that American dream does get out of control – anyone who lived and traded through a financial crisis can attest to that. Front office, as it turns out, is a surprisingly more athletic place than one might first imagine; so to meet the demands of trading, it makes a lot of sense to make sure that you are shooting the lights out not just mentally, but physically, in the way that you train to meet the demands of your vocation.

> Trading, it is not often appreciated, is a physical activity, a demanding one, so the important effects of testosterone might be physical; rather than cognitive. High testosterone levels or increased androgenic effects, for example, can increase vigilance and visuo-motor skills such as scanning and speed of reactions . . . qualities that may help traders to spot and trade price discrepancies before others arbitrage them away.
>
> (Coates et al., 2010, p. 337)

Exercise is an opioid that offers a powerful natural high, or euphoria, which is the first persuasive reason to choose it. It is so powerful, in fact, that 'even a single bout of it, can have a robust prophylactic effect against the build-up of anger' (Eisold, 2010). Exercise has been statistically shown to improve cognitive reasoning, executive and top-down cognitive control when executing a task (Hillman et al., 2008). Habitual exercise also predicts freedom from depression (e.g. in an eight-year study; Salmon, 2001) and limits feelings of panic when we are fearful (Clark, 1986). Strength training reduces depression in patients undergoing drug detoxification, whereas aerobic training does not (Palmer et al., 1995). The cessation of regular running caused depression and anxiety to reappear in people with an existing emotional disorder after only two weeks (Peter et al., 2000). Habitual exercisers are, on the whole, less stressed, with business executives who had undergone a big life-changing stressful event reporting a greater capability to handle the stress if they exercised regularly (Kobasa et al., 1985) – even in extreme situations such as a recent HIV diagnosis (LaPerriere et al., 1990). The effect can be almost immediate, with personal problems reported as being less serious after just one walk (Thayer, 1987; see also '#10 The power of nature'), and as 'perturbed homeostatic mechanisms [return] toward the normal physiological range . . . daily physical activity normalises gene expression' (Booth et al., 2002, p. 399.). Professor Jim Pfaus notes that 'by activating our arousal and attention systems, stressors can wake up the neural circuitry underlying wanting and craving, just like drugs do' (Schreiber, 2012). Exercise also activates those same systems, waking up the same neural circuitry.

Exercise also increases serotonin, partly because of its role in heightening levels of tryptophan, a serotonin precursor, in the brain (Young, 2007). This could be considered an important effect given one observation of a negative association between dietary tryptophan and suicide rates (Voracek & Tran, 2007) and the elevated incidence of depression and suicide amongst finance professionals.

Two things are largely going to dictate how effectively someone deals with stress – how constructively they view the situation and how physically healthy they are (Flier & Underhill, 1998). For traders, training like an athlete makes perfect sense – for example, if one observes the increase that takes place in cardiovascular tone of a trader's body following a day of trading in volatile markets (Lo & Repin, 2002). 'The endocrine system may be the missing link in the new field of neuroscience and economics, connecting market events to brain processes' (Caldú & Dreher, 2007, cited in Coates et al., 2010, p. 340). We now know that anticipating trades invokes 'anticipation anxiety', which adds to allostatic load and needs to be managed out by positive lifestyle choices, including regular exercise and a good diet.

Most people know about the 'runner's high' already – the short-term euphoria caused by a great cardio workout – but there is so much more to the story.

Firstly, several euphoriants exist within the body – not only endorphins. This includes phenethylamine (a stimulant), anandamine (a cannabinoid) and the previously noted endorphin (an opioid). Exercising with others can also involve oxytocin (a 'binding' hormone that helps us fall in love). Exercise also enhances serotonin and norepinephrine, two brain monoamines that play a crucial role in the positive effects of BDNF (brain-derived neurotrophic factor) and in promoting general feelings of well-being.

Phenethylamine is potent and reacts in the central nervous system in the same way as amphetamines; it also mediates the euphoric effects of the well-known 'runner's high'. Just one decent cardio workout can result in the experience of a better mood for the entire day, so exercising in the morning is often preferable.

Strenuous aerobic exercise has an analgesic effect, with opioid responses to exercise providing an inhibitory effect on the body's stress response. If exercise is habitual, the body becomes better at this process, with our plasma beta-endorphin responses increasing during exercise as we become more well-trained over time (Carr et al., 1981). But it is not just important to exercise to reduce a stress response: it is also important to exercise to respond more quickly and effectively. Crucial to financial markets participants is the fact that regular aerobic exercise exerts a powerful combative effect on addictive behaviour by altering FoSB or FoSsC (transcriptional regulators of stress and anti-depressant responses) immunoreactivity in the striatum and in other parts of the brain's reward system. Individuals who engage in regular aerobic exercise are less likely to engage in drug self-administration, and are less likely to relapse (e.g. Daniel et al., 2006; Prochaska et al., 2008). Furthermore, aerobic exercise induces opposite effects of dopamine receptors to those induced by several types of addictive drugs. FoSB expression in the nucleus accumbens is also crucial for its effect on improving resilience to stress (Wallace et al., 2008).

Financial markets participants are constantly exposed to stress, given the cortisol-raising uncertainty, fragility and volatility of the markets within which they trade. They are also exposed to potentially addiction-inducing triggers within their roles (e.g. trading can become addictive, mimicking in some ways the act of gambling). This exposes them to greater vulnerability to addictive behaviours: 'exposure to stimulants and/or stress cumulatively, while enhancing dopamine release in striatal areas, may contribute to a lowered set point for psychopathologies in which altered dopamine neurotransmission is invoked' (Booij et al., 2016, p. 1). Thus, the anti-addictive properties of exercise represent a powerful weapon for financial markets participants in the fight against the development of an unhealthy reliance on trading or investing for non-P&L (i.e. addictive)-related reasons.

Physically active people also exhibit lower levels of anxiety and depression, partly due to the effects of exercise on norepinephrine, which helps the brain cope more effectively with stress. Fifty per cent of the brain's neuromodulator norepinephrine is produced in an area of the brain called the locus coeruleus, which plays a major role in modulating the body's stress response. The neurobiological effects of exercise are, in sum, profound, with only 30 minutes of cardiovascular exercise a day creating significant changes in behaviour, neural plasticity, memory, mood and productivity, creating short-term euphoria and lessening desire for other addictive or pleasure-seeking behaviours, and upregulating DHEA and BDNF production (neurotrophic factors that enhance intelligence and feelings of well-being), particularly in the prefrontal cortex, anterior cingulate, caudate nucleus and hippocampus (allowing better executive control over our emotions).

> Our feelings of engagement and excitement as we seek the material resources needed for bodily survival, and also when we pursue the cognitive interests that bring positive existential meanings into our lives . . . [without dopamine] human aspirations remain frozen . . . is it any wonder that humans and animals eagerly work to artificially activate this system whether via electrical or chemical means?
>
> (Panksepp, 2004, p. 144)

Exercise significantly improves our ability to process conflicting sources of data without experiencing cognitive dissonance, strengthens executive and top-down control and leaves us, as a result, less exposed to the phenomenon of *hot cognition* (Thagard, 2003) – a tendency for reasoning to be governed far more strongly by the emotional, as opposed to rational, area of the brain.

Exercise significantly increases brain concentrations of norepinephrine, alongside a host of other positive adaptations. The pleasant experience of exercising is so strong, in fact, that exercising together has caused couples to feel more satisfied and in love after undertaking a physical challenge together (Aron et al., 2000). The physiological arousal of exercise seems to create sensations of romantic attraction (Lewandowski et al., 2004), and people can as a result mistake the physiological arousal of exercise for romantic attraction (Dutton & Aron, 1974). The nonverbal matching of two people performing the same exercises can also enhance feelings of attraction (Stel & Vonk, 2010). Working out with a spouse can therefore not only induce greater trading benefits but also increase the quality of your relationship.

Ultimately, endurance exercise offers positive routes to the achievement of an opioid, amphetamine-like high, satiating the brain's need for dopamine, restoring damage, minimising overemotional behaviours and meaning that the 'drug hit' that we get from exercise lowers our need for dangerous risk-taking, addiction and sensation-seeking. These outcomes translate to better, more rational trading and ultimately optimisation of P&L as a result.

#2 Anabolic arbitrage: lift heavy to trade smart

> There are grounds for believing that the emotions of euphoria and fear displayed in markets may be more accurately described as shifts in confidence and risk preferences, ones caused by elevated levels of steroid hormones.
>
> — Coates et al. (2010, p. 331)

When you think of steroids, what immediately comes to mind? Most likely Arnold Schwarzenegger, Pumping Iron and bodybuilders. But what we know is that all traders and investors – all financial markets participants – also depend on their own endogenous (i.e. naturally occurring) steroidal hormones to mediate feelings of fear, anger and aggression, to moderate risk-taking decisions, to possess the courage and strength to act in the face of tough opposition, and to sustain a strong search preference and focus. What is less well-known is the fundamental role that strength training plays in maintaining the body's equilibrium, or *homeostasis* (most people are only aware of the runner's high). Maximising P&L is a step closer to those who lift.

Testosterone, for example, downregulates cortisol, which is why a great heavy lifting session in the gym or a boxing session hitting the pads can make you feel so much calmer. Weight training also significantly raises GABA (Gamma Aminobutyric Acid) levels, an extremely useful side effect, as high levels of the neurotransmitter GABA produce feelings of calm and improve focus. Conversely, low levels can trigger anxiety.

Excess testosterone can lead to over-trading and aggression. It is necessary for testosterone to be controlled: strength training is by far the most effective route to controlling testosterone levels. Increased testosterone increases the growth hormone response, and both positively influence the release of insulin-like growth factor. Weight training also activates the adrenal glands (glucocorticoids – cortisol; catecholamine – adrenaline, norepinephrine, dopamine; and mineralocorticoids – sodium), which help to regulate stress. Further, in a 2010 study (O'Connor et al., 2010), resistance training was reported to increase executive function, memory and cognition, as well as reduce depression, with 94% of 70 randomized studies reported in the study showing that exercise is clinically beneficial (i.e. significant), more so than drug or cognitive–behavioural interventions in treating depression and fatigue. Interestingly, strength training-only interventions produced the largest improvements in chronic fatigue. The same study also reported that resistance training over an 8–10-week period cause a 30% reduction in sleep disorders amongst depressed individuals (the 8–10 weeks of consistent training was a minimum required time for positive changes to occur).

The demands of ancient Palaeolithic life required the regular lifting of heavy objects, with development of substantive skeletal muscle a favoured pre-reproductive survival trait (Booth et al., 2002). A failure to maintain substantive skeletal muscular strength subsequently interferes with the delicate ability of our bodies to achieve the complexities of a homeostatic state, as the genomic modifications of Palaeolithic times assumed a level of muscularity for optimal functioning to occur. It could be argued that subsequently, 'for those interested in the health and well-being of humankind, a basic understanding of evolutionary pressures that have shaped human physiological responses to the environment is a necessity' (Gerber & Crews, 1999, cited in Booth et al., 2002, p. 407).

The physiological responses necessary for Wall Street executives include the need for both muscular and cardiovascular strength so that homeostasis is most easily achieved, so that neurogenesis and the repair and protection of existing grey matter is optimised, so that cognitive reaction and processing speeds are quickest, and so that executives are able to maintain the stamina needed to perform optimally, day after day.

Moderate volume, high intensity training increases testosterone, growth hormones, and IGF-1 (insulin-like growth factor, which stimulates physical growth during childhood and helps build and repair muscle tissue in adults). In the short term, strength training lowers testosterone and increases cortisol, but if adequate rest is provided following training, a compensatory anabolic state occurs and levels return to normal. It has been observed that 'exercise, fitness, and many of the drugs used to build mass also have a fortunate consequence of lowering cortisol levels' (Gwartney, 2009), and it is fascinating that raising testosterone levels through lifting weights has the effect of inhibiting the response of our adrenal glands to ACTH (a hormone released in response to stress that tells our brain to release cortisol). The net effect of this interaction is that we produce less cortisol under stress. Growth hormone, also produced through lifting weights, prevents cortisol from being reactivated from its inactive form (cortisone).

Strength training specifically has been observed to reduce depression in patients undergoing drug detoxification (Palmer et al., 1995), whilst the cessation of regular running caused depression and anxiety to reappear in people with an existing emotional disorder after only two weeks of inactivity (Peter et al., 2000).

#3 Working out makes you smarter

> No man has the right to be an amateur in the matter of physical training.
> — Socrates (Xenophon, 1994)

John Urschel is 6'3", over 300 pounds and shoots the lights out as an offensive lineman for the Baltimore Ravens. Urschel is well documented as being able to lift heavy – 225 pounds bench press for 30 reps – and he can run fast – a 40 yard dash in 5.2 seconds. This year Urschel is switching direction to commence a PhD in Mathematics at MIT, having recently co-authored the *Journal of Computational Mathematics*-published 'A Cascadic Multigrid Algorithm for Computing the Fiedler Vector of Graph Laplacians'

(Urschel et al., 2014). The absolute irony of this chapter, with reference to the impressive anecdote of Urschel, is that athletes are often viewed as being not very bright, with highly intelligent individuals often viewed as not-very-athletic. This book bursts with scientific data supporting the premise that maximisation of cognitive ability and execution of task is *only* possible when our brain chemistry is optimal, and that optimal state can only really be achieved with a dedication to honouring the Palaeolithic genomic requirements of our ancestors – by exercising regularly, by eating right and by resting when we need to. A strong body leads to a strong mind. Urschel's example is entertaining because it is surprising, but such surprise is wholly irrational: science tells us it is more probable than not for Urschel to be cognitively more able with exercise than without.

An amazing outcome of strength training is its key role in the increased expression and synthesis of brain-derived neurotrophic factor (BDNF), which improves mood, memory and cognitive function, neurogenesis, neural plasticity and neural repair. Moderate to high intensity aerobic exercise can lead to an amazing three-fold increase in BDNF levels. Exercise also significantly increases levels of serum IGF-1, a neurotrophic factor that works alongside BDNF to enhance neurogenesis and neuroplasticity. As exercise duration and intensity increases, so does the level of IGF-1 increase. Exercise also increases signalling of the protein VEGF, which protects neurons, improves cerebral blood flow and contributes to hippocampal neurogenesis. Whilst BDNF expression is a critical outcome of cardiovascular exercise, it is also highly involved in the positive outcomes of resistance training (e.g. Yarrow et al., 2010).

CEO of JP Morgan Jamie Dimon once told his daughter, in response to her question 'What is a financial crisis?', that it is 'something that happens every 5–7 years' (Sundby, 2010). The kind of panic, fear and euphoria wrought by these pro-cyclical boom-and-bust scenarios are emotionally and cognitively debilitating. As Dr Rajita Sinha, Professor of Psychiatry and Neurobiology at Yale, noted, 'over time, as the number of cumulative stressors increases, chronic stress can interact with that and worsen the effect' (Park, 2012). Warren Buffett (The Warren Buffett Way, 2013) hangs his metaphorical coat on the ability to sit back and reflect; but he owns his own company, has no manager barking down his neck to dump stock when the markets tank, and he is not under the exceptional pressure and fear of being fired that most institutional actors experience:

> I insist on a lot of time being spent, almost every day, to just sit and think. That is very uncommon in American business. I read and think. So I do more reading and thinking, and make less impulse decisions than most people in business.

The kind of chronic stress identified by Dr Sinha can cause the death of brain tissue, anxiety, depression, loss aversion or overly risky trading. Of the many, many benefits of exercise, neurogenesis and the ability to practice better executive control (a requirement in a financial crisis) stands out as two of the most valuable:

> Collectively, convergent evidence supports the view that higher levels of physical activity correlate with increased top-down control, which could be mediated through more efficient activation of the ACC, resulting in better performance during tasks requiring executive control.
>
> (Hillman et al., 2008, p. 58)

It also passes on an incredible view of exercise as a weapon that we can use to practice our stress response on: 'Although repeated exposure to uncontrollable stressors eventually produces resistance to stress, exposure to controllable stress achieves this more quickly' (Salmon, 2001, pp. 50–51).

#4 Hedge your exposure to stress and go long on sleep

Money never sleeps.
— *Wall Street: Money Never Sleeps* (2010)

Money might not sleep, but traders and investors should. And they should get a lot more of it if they want to maximise P&L. As value investor Seth Klarman so sagely noted, 'one risk-related consideration should be paramount above all others: the ability to sleep well at night, confident that your financial position is secure whatever the future may bring' (Klarman, Preface to Graham & Dodd, 2009).

Not sleeping enough increases cortisol levels, decreases leptin, a hormone that regulates appetite via feelings of satiety, and upregulates ghrelin (which increases appetite): this is one reason why being tired leads to eating sugar and junk food. Aside from also risking a greater likelihood of Type II diabetes, impaired sleep also messes with cognitive function and mood. Sleep-deprived individuals, for example, exhibit amygdala activation up to 60% higher when faced with an emotion-inducing trigger, risking overreactions such as over-trading, over-optimism or loss aversion, because a loss of sleep disrupts the connection between the amygdala and the medial prefrontal cortex, the area of our brains that regulate responses from the amygdala. In fact, a 2011 study (Venkatraman et al., 2011) found that people made riskier and overly optimistic gambling choices when sleep deprived. Even one bad night of sleep exerts a detrimental effect on memory, with sleep mediating our ability to integrate new data with existing knowledge (Tamminen et al., 2013), and with high baseline sleep spindle activity linked to a higher IQ (Fogel et al., 2007).

As stress increases cortisol, and cortisol raises the risk of emotional trading and investing, it is crucial that financial markets participants prioritise the minimisation of cortisol levels, and engage in exercise to reverse the brain damage caused by stress. Sleep is just as important as exercise in this regard:

> The interplay between stress and sleep impacts BDNF levels, suggesting an important role of this relationship in the pathogenesis of stress-associated mental disorders. Hence, we suggest sleep as a key mediator at the connection between stress and BDNF. Whether sleep is maintained or disturbed might explain why some individuals are able to handle a certain stress load while others develop a mental disorder.
>
> (Giese et al., 2013, p. 1)

Lack of sleep also significantly lowers testosterone, which is a problem for traders and investors: high testosterone levels were positively correlated with P&L in one study (Coates et al., 2010), but a fall in testosterone can negatively affect feelings of well-being (Leproult & Van Cauter, 2011), and testosterone is needed to downregulate cortisol.

A study by Harvard Medical School and the University of California, Berkeley (as reported in Cell Press, 2007) found sleep to be 'a biological necessity, and without it, there is only so far the band will stretch before it snaps, with both cognitive and emotional consequences'. Even the researchers conducting the study were amazed by the results, stating

> We had predicted a potential increase in the emotional reaction from the brain [in people deprived of sleep], but the size of the increase truly surprised us. [. . .] The emotional centers of the brain were over 60% more reactive under conditions of sleep deprivation than in subjects who had obtained a normal night of sleep. It is almost as though, without sleep, the brain reverts back to a more primitive pattern of activity, becoming unable to put emotional experiences into context and produce controlled, appropriate responses.

Aside from sleep, pastimes aimed at increasing relaxation and lowering cortisol include yoga (e.g. Thirthalli et al., 2013; Cell Press, 2007). Breathing exercises, meditation and stretching also induce positive relaxation-related benefits. Regular massages, for example, provide a great route to relaxation. For example, a review of studies of massage therapy reported significant decreases in cortisol levels of up to 31% in massage therapy recipients, and an average increase of 28% and 31% in serotonin and dopamine levels.

Imposing bans on Blackberries and other mobile and electronic devices give time for the mind to wind down. A recent Harvard Medical School study, for example, found that exposure to technology before sleeping interferes significantly with melatonin onset and release) (Rose, 2015). The National Sleep Foundation recommends turning off all technology an hour prior to sleep given its negative effects on sleep and brain function, including the impact on melatonin, and the utilisation of orange screens is recommended to minimise melatonin-disrupting effects. The use of orange screens for traders and investors on trading floors is becoming increasingly popular. Excessive tech use can lead to abnormally high brain arousal, making us feel 'wired and tired' (Dunckley, 2011).

The positive stress-reducing effects of exercise can be almost immediate, with personal problems reported as being less serious after just one walk (Thayer, 1987). Exercise, for example, has been statistically shown to improve cognitive reasoning, executive and top-down cognitive control when executing a task (Hillman et al., 2008). Habitual exercise also predicts freedom from depression (e.g. in an eight-year study by Salmon (2001)) and limits feelings of panic when we are fearful (Clark, 1986).

Something as simple as taking a few moments to engage in deep breathing can exert a profound effect on performance. A recent academic study reports that 175 neurons located in the brain's breathing centre (the pre-Bötzinger complex) tell the body to 'calm down' when breathing becomes slower (Garcia et al., 2011). This is primarily achieved by engaging the body's parasympathetic nervous system – in particular, the Vagus nerve – which significantly slows down and dampens the effects of an adrenaline inducing, excitatory response (e.g. shaking hands, dry mouth, common symptoms of panic that will affect performance, like before a big presentation). A second one is to switch off social media and let your mind simply take in the sights and sounds around you; you will be less likely to feel angry, lost or frustrated if you do (Krasnova et al., 2013).

Although the Olympic marathon runners of 1908 drank cognac to improve performance (Grandjean, 1997, 877S), sport science has thankfully advanced in leaps and bounds since then. The financial markets can, similarly, make great leaps and bounds in the way in which it trains traders and investors to achieve peak performance, particularly in the management of stress, if the observations identified in this chapter are adopted.

#5 Hungry for success? Eat right to trade and invest better

Gimme guys who are poor, smart and hungry.

— Gordon Gekko, *Wall Street* (1987)

Specific supplements, vitamins and minerals exert a really positive effect on our brain chemistry, including the maximisation of dopamine and other 'happy' hormones. Specifically, B-vitamins and omega oils play a decisive role in promoting a better mood, feelings of well-being and happiness. For example, a recent study of EPA (eicosapentaenoic acid, a form of Omega-3 fatty acid) use concluded that 'EPA-rich supplementation, participants' brains worked "less hard" and achieved a better cognitive performance than prior to supplementation' (Bauer et al., 2014) and found that Vitamin B5 (panthethine), specifically, is effective in dealing with a hypersecretion of cortisol. 'Our findings indicate the importance of training the dopamine system to accurately assess risk and reward in the context of trading' (Sapra et al., 2012, p. 1). Eating adequate amounts of undamaged Omega oils is essential for brain health – great sources include almonds, sunflower seeds, oily fish and flax. However, given the importance of balancing Omega-3, 6 and 9 sources, a supplement such as Udo's Choice oils that offer an optimised balance is recommended.

Whilst supplements such acetyl- L-Carnitine (ALC) and high protein intake are more traditionally found in bodybuilding and fitness magazines, they do also present compelling benefits to stressed-out executives. For example, ALC has been shown to demonstrate significant anti-depressant outcomes effects in only one week, in addition to leading to improvements in attention, concentration, psychomotor speed, memory and concentration.[1] Tryptophan, an amino acid, is also found abundantly in high protein foods, and it is vital that an adequate intake of protein occurs alongside the ingestion of healthy carbohydrates and good fats such as EPAs as a result. The reason that tryptophan is so valuable is because it plays a vital role in the creation of by-product 5HTP (5-hydroxytryptophan), which produces feelings of well-being and calm, increases energy, lowers anxiety, boosts happiness and enhances sleep quality by increasing production of serotonin.

A common mistake of dieters is to lower calories and carbohydrates too sharply, cutting off the brain's supply of serotonin, which makes them turn to sugar, chocolate and other comfort foods to get a serotonin rush back into their brain. A far more efficient route to health, even fat loss (which also keeps vital serotonin/5-HTP levels high),[2] is to keep healthy carbohydrates relatively high alongside a decent protein and healthy fat intake, and to engage in weight and cardio training to make the body leaner. 5-HTP actually plays a crucial role in many treatments for depression. Supplements containing tryptophan can exert positive effects on mild-to-moderate depression (Young, 2007) – whilst foods high in tryptophan are often recommended, diet-based tryptophan is usually less effective as it does not cross the blood–brain barrier.

Magnesium, referred to by *Psychology Today* as 'the original chill pill' (Deans, 2011), also possesses powerful anti-depressant properties, partly because it suppresses the release of ACTH (adrenocorticotrophic hormone), which is vital in stimulating the adrenal glands to release cortisol and adrenaline. A relationship between magnesium deficiency and pathological anxiety has been found in clinical trials (e.g. Sartori et al., 2012), with a dysregulation in the HPA axis (hypothalamic–pituitary–adrenocortical) axis, contributing to hyper-emotionality in response to a dietary-induced state of hypomagnesaemia (magnesium deficiency) (ibid.). This role it exerts on the HPA is a critical factor as the HPA axis constitutes our body's main stress response system. A lack of calcium and D3 has also been found to contribute significantly to mood disturbances, with iron deficiency linked to some psychiatric disorders, as iron deficiency impairs the development of emotional regulation and cognition (Chen et al., 2013). A good multi-mineral supplement thus represents a healthy, positive addition to anyone's daily routine.

As high stress levels can cause digestive disruption, supplements that assist in gut function are advisable for many people. For example, L-glutamine is advised for many people who suffer from digestive disorders given its positive effect on gut restoration. The body's immunological response is affected massively by gut health, making it a key focus for any stressed-out executive who experiences 'leisure sickness' on a regular basis (i.e. getting sick at weekends or vacation periods as soon as you take a rest, as your adrenals will stop pumping out adrenaline to keep you 'running-on-empty'). Taking probiotics, digestive enzymes and/or acidophilus and limiting sugar and caffeine represent a solid strategy in maintaining good gut health, which will lead to less illnesses (the gut actually houses between 70 and 80% of the body's entire immune cells) (Furness et al., 1999).

Junk food, conversely, affects the brain extremely negatively, with allostatic load (as discussed in Chapter 3) invoked far more quickly in the presence of a high fat or high sugar diet. Firstly, excessive consumption of either can blunt serotonin sensitivity by overstimulating serotonin pathways, playing a role in addiction, anxiety and depression. Short-term effects in over-ingestion of sugar include irritability, anger, frustration, mood swings and anxiety and can impair cognitive function due to the effects of a 'sugar crash' on insulin.

Sugary junk food has been shown, in fact, to be as addictive as cocaine (Payton, 2016): in 2015, Dr James DiNicolantonio published a review of the dangers of sugar, which included the statement that 'when you look at animal studies comparing sugar to cocaine, even when you get the rats hooked on IV cocaine, once you introduce sugar, almost all of them switch to the sugar'.

Ever seen an angry trader throw his phone across the desk or shout at someone? This is one outcome of fluctuating serotonin levels caused by not eating regularly enough, not intaking enough calories, restricting carbohy-drates too far (e.g. a Paleo or Atkins diet) or as a result of stress (cortisol downregulates serotonin). It is subsequently recommended that traders and investors eat very healthy food every 3–4 hours, which would be optimal for keeping blood sugar, alertness, mood and energy in check.

Coffee (caffeine) has both positive and negative outcomes, depending on how much you drink. Caffeine essentially competes with a neurotrans-mitter adenosine, which is responsible for modulating attention, alertness and sleep. When adenosine levels drop, we feel fatigued and sleepy. Coffee can increase learning in the short-term and stimulate glutamate, serotonin and dopamine, which increase feelings of well-being. However, overuse can cause insomnia, anxiety, irritability, an upset stomach, rapid heartbeat and muscle tremors. Its use as a performance aid in small doses is therefore viable, but overuse is dangerous.

Generally, a bad diet (e.g. Popkin, 2006) can exert a powerful and extremely debilitating effect on mental health (e.g. it even plays a role in the development of some psychiatric diseases; see Kroll, 2007), includ-ing the ability to cope with stress. Even taking a multivitamin once a day seems to produce positive benefits. As reported in a scientific study of the use of Berocca, a popular (and relatively high-dose) multivitamin, 'relative to placebo, treatment with Berocca was associated with consist-ent and statistically significant reductions in anxiety and perceived stress. Participants in the Berocca group also tended to rate themselves as less tired and better able to concentrate following treatment' (Carroll, 2000). Daily use of a multivitamin is therefore suggested as a simple means of optimising diet.

#6 Use music as a performance tool

> As long as the music is playing, you've got to get up and dance.
> — Chuck Prince, Citigroup CEO (Financial Crisis Inquiry Commission, 2010)

Chuck Prince got into a lot of trouble for his choice of wording during post-2008 regulatory investigation hearings. Yet the metaphor is remarkably on point. Music really sways sentiment and has the power to tip a trader into over-emotional states if its timing and use, particularly alongside other stimulatory phenomena, is mistimed or misappreciated. Take John Thomas Financial Inc., run by Anastasios 'Tommy' Belesis, where each trader walks past a huge statue of a bull as they enter the building (the offices were based in a prestigious location opposite the NYSE, where Belesis's Rolls Royce was often parked outside), whose vending machine stocked only Red Bull, and who practice sales pitches to the heavy thud of the *Rocky* soundtrack. It represented a literal testosterone pre-fight pump-up locker room of an organisation. The culmination of high natural morning testosterone levels in traders, the stimulatory effects of Red Bull, the emotive and rousing soundtrack of *Rocky* (and the mental imagery of fighting that it evokes) and the huge bull statue all push up testosterone levels, which can quickly lead to overly risky trading and a greater likelihood of opportunistic trading and fraud. This is more a route to sensation-seeking than rational trading. Belesis (perhaps unsurprisingly, given what we now know about the role of physiology in trading) became subject to an SEC and FINRA investigation and was subsequently barred from the securities industry in January 2015.

Music can actually be used as a functional tool to manipulate neural activation. This kind of self-regulation listening to music can allow you to start and end the day during your commute with a modulated response to stress (e.g. Moore, 2013), as music actually induces specific mood states via stimulation of neural areas responsible for the processing of emotions (e.g. Koelsch, 2010). Listening to sad or discordant music with one's eyes closed, for example, enhances amygdala activation (Lerner, 2009), strengthening its effects, whilst pairing the music with imagery enhanced effects even further. Sad music should be avoided on this basis, as it increases feelings of discord (Mitterschiffthaler et al., 2007).

Pleasant, energetic and familiar music, conversely, activated the ACC (anterior cingulate cortex), the OFC (orbitofrontal cortex) and the LPFC (lateral prefrontal cortex), with preferred musical choices energising the brain's reward function. These areas need to be as strong and as switched on as possible – every day – as they represent the cognitive control function of your brain. This cognitive control centre lowers amygdala activity (the knee-jerk emotional response that can cause herding, overtrading, fear, etc.). Music thus represents an excellent means of manipulating the strength of our cognitive control function and minimising the strength of our emotional (and thus irrational) impulses.

#7 Harness the power of nature

> Someone's sitting in the shade today because someone planted a tree a long time ago.
>
> —Warren Buffett (cited in Kilpatrick, 1992, p. 288)

Exercising in nature carries significant emotional, mental and physical benefits, regardless of level, type, duration or intensity, including reductions in anger, confusion, depression and anxiety (Pretty et al., 2003, 2005, 2007; Morris, 2003; Pacione, 2003), increased happiness (Mäler et al., 2008), better emotional well-being (Kuo & Sullivan, 2001), mental and physical fitness (Scully et al., 19989; Rubinstein, 1997), self-esteem (Pretty et al., 2007), a reduction of mental stress (Pretty, 2004; Ulrich, 2002; Laumann, 2003; Grahn & Stigsdotter, 2003), mindfulness and calm (Brymer et al., 2014), a decreased risk of mental illness (de Vries et al., 2003) and less frustration and greater work satisfaction (Tennessen & Cimprich, 1995). It also lessens mental fatigue (de Vries et al., 2003), leads to better sleep (Astell et al., 2013) and promotes faster recovery from illness.

The restorative properties for urban dwellers appear striking (e.g. Ulrich, 1979, 1981, 1984, 2002; Ulrich et al., 1991), and many authors suggest that nature-based scenes carry such a strong psychological impact that simply viewing photographs of nature can alleviate stress (e.g. Morris, 2003; Ulrich, 1984; Kaplan & Norton, 1992; Ulrich & Parsons, 1992; White & Heerwagen, 1998). Thus, simply adding images of nature to your desk, office walls and PC background offer an impactful stress release.

Exercising outside also increases levels of vitamin D and serotonin, further compounding positive psychological outcomes. As Young (2007, p. 395) states, there is a 'a positive correlation between serotonin synthesis and the hours of sunlight in the day' – which is particularly valuable for institutional traders and investors to know, as they generally tend to suffer from a lack of exposure to bright light, and this lack of exposure places them at greater risk of depression (Lambert, 2006).

Exercising outdoors 'produces greater physiological changes toward relaxation, greater changes to positive emotions and vitality, and faster recovery of attention-demanding cognitive performances' (Korpela et al., 2014, p. 2). Given that it is perhaps cognitive restoration, as opposed to exercise itself, that provides the greatest benefits of outdoor exercise, it is recommended that the reader engage at least once a week in any activity that involves extensive exposure to nature.

#8 We are hardwired to herd

> The financial markets offer many temptations to vulnerable investors. It is easy to do the wrong thing, to speculate rather than invest. Emotion lies dangerously close to the surface for most investors and can be particularly intense when market prices move dramatically in either direction.
> — Seth Klarman (1991, p. 31)

We are evolutionarily designed to socially conform or – in trading parlance – to *herd*. Protecting young traders and investors from these kinds of evolutionary urges may represent a particularly crucial goal for the HR or managerial functions of financial institutions, as young traders' brains predispose them far more greatly to making mistakes and exercising poor judgement. This is because the prefrontal cortex (the impulse-control centre of the brain) does not reach full maturity until 25 years of age.

Given that money exerts a seductive effect, that excitation-transfer spreads emotions across a trading floor and that the financial markets tend to reify those traders that make the largest profits, it is easy to see how all traders can get caught up in the heady upswing or panic-inducing tailspin of a boom-and-bust scenario. Perhaps, given the relative immaturity of a young trader's brain, the socialisation effect might render him more susceptible to future emotional and irrational behaviours, including opportunistic trading.

#9 Embrace hedonism

> Nature has placed mankind under the governance of two sovereign masters, pain and pleasure.
>
> — J. Bentham (1823, p. 1)

If the quasi-fictional worlds of *Wall Street* (1987), *Margin Call* (2011), *The Big Short* (2015) and *Wolf of Wall Street* (2013) are to be believed, Wall Street is a hedonistic place. Embracing hedonism enables traders and investors to be honest about the emotions that drive them and to find effective ways of managing them. As noted by Lloyd Blankfein, CEO of Goldman Sachs, 'sentiment has a real effect. This is not natural science. It's a social science, so sentiment and people's feeling really matters' (Sandholm, 2013). It really is true that emotions drive us – evolutionary science, physiology and sport science tell us in an incredibly clear message that this is the case. What is truly significant to this book is that emotions such as greed and fear can even be mapped on to physiological reactions such as muscular contractions.

> The basic emotions affecting valuation, fear and greed, are related to very specific muscular configurations. To each of them corresponds a pattern of muscular contraction without which it has no existence. Fear is associated with the withdrawal reflex, also known as the startle response, in which the anterior flexor muscles are contracted, curling the body. In contrast, greed is assertive and related to the action response, which contracts the posterior extensor muscles, lifting and

arching the back. A biased market participant lacks awareness: the capacity to make sensory-motor shifts.

(Cymbalista, 2003, p. 32)

Herding impulses that drive the creation and perpetuation of damaging boom-and-bust scenarios also appear to originate in our limbic system, so we need to be able to first recognise, then manage, these reactions to avoid a tendency to herd:

> The mass psychological aspect of trend formation is related to herding impulses involved in the limbic system, the part of the brain that involves emotions and motivation. Even though most people do not know how to work with it, the capacity to recognise such patterns is instinctive, a mechanism with which evolution has endowed us to handle complex and uncertain social situations.

(Cymbalista, 2003, p. 32)

When viewed in this way – that trading impulses have physiological origin and signalling – George Soros's legendary 'backache' as a trigger to trade suddenly stops sounding weird and starts sounding pretty scientific. Soros believes that he receives as many useful signals from his backaches as he does from theory, a belief supported by the idea that 'Soros' backache works as a barometer (Cymbalista, 2003, p. 37).Backaches are a key symptom of adrenal fatigue and allostatic load, which one would reasonably expect a long-term investor to exhibit. Soros's respect for physiological signals are part of what makes him successful.

We also know that money seduces us all, to the point where it is, arguably, impossible to trade rationally. To acknowledge this is to embrace it. It also enables the reader to honestly appraise, without shame, how vulnerable they are, as an individual, to the threat of addiction and opportunistic trading, and to subsequently engage as effectively as possible with the lifestyle changes that will allow them to manage these risks.

What can we take away from this? Fundamentally, that the orthodox economics position of *homo economicus* is too narrow, and we need to start embracing what makes us human in order to fully maximise profitable outcomes for all traders and investors. Just as an athlete manipulates his physiology to perform at an elite level and win gold, traders can, similarly, learn to manipulate their own reactions.

#10 Willpower is finite; use it wisely

It is no difficult trick to bring a great deal of energy, study, and native ability into Wall Street and to end up with losses instead of profits. These virtues, if channeled in the wrong directions, become indistinguishable from handicaps.

— Benjamin Graham (1949, p. 8)

Self-control and will-power are necessary skills in trading. The good news is that our self-control is adaptive, meaning we can improve it through training. However, that bad news is that your will-power is *finite*. And that is very bad news for traders and investors.

The fast-paced, 24/7 nature of trading is something that the Palaeolithic brain was simply not designed to cope with, leading to many side-effects associated with over-stimulation (e.g. adrenal fatigue, stress addiction). Throw too many decisions at your brain over a short period of time (e.g. a high volume of trades), and you will experience decision fatigue, leading to sub-par quality decisions; throw too many demands at your brain to exert willpower, and your willpower will actually run out. This is very relevant to traders and investors, who constantly need to flex their willpower, given the many, many factors that are constantly pushing us to react emotionally (which consequently runs the risk of emotional – and therefore unprofitable – trading). As we know, these scenarios include the seductive effect of money on the brain, the negative effect of unpredictability of cortisol levels, the overly risk trading decisions that can be caused by testosterone (androgenic priming and the winner effect), our evolutionary predilection to herd, the dominance of our emotional brain in reacting to stressful or demanding situations, and a heightened vulnerability to addiction, anxiety and depression for financial markets participants.

New York Times writer John Tierney noted in a review of willpower-focused studies that 'willpower turned out to be more than a folk concept or a metaphor. It really was a form of mental energy that could be exhausted'. Interestingly, one of the ways that willpower can be improved is to make sure that you are eating healthily. The brain uses around 25% of our bodies' circulating glucose, and if we eat too infrequently, or too little, we produce too little glucose – which has been shown in studies to negatively impact willpower (McGonigal, 2011). Lower glucose levels also seem to heighten our stress response to outside stimuli, which can further impair judgement and contribute to decision-fatigue. Subsequently, eating around every 3–4 hrs and relying on a healthy diet with an intake of moderate–low (as opposed to high) energy release carbohydrates, combined with good fats, fibre and protein, will ensure that blood glucose levels remain stable. Further, minimising stimulation (e.g. no tech use at home, or during a work commute, where possible), trying to slow down significantly the pace of life during one's leisure time, and building breaks in at work (even a coffee break and a brief walk around the block) will provide a much-needed mental break.

Trader physiology: key takeaways

- All of the negative effects of stress that a trader and investor are exposed to can be reversed completely via the utilisation of exercise (both strength and aerobics training are necessary for optimised results);
- Trading and investing practices can be optimised via the manipulation of physiological variables (e.g. cortisol, oxytocin, serotonin, testosterone, GABA, DHEA, endorphins) as an optimised physiological state enables optimised cognitive and physical functions;
- Trading and investing is a physical vocation in many ways – as studies of trader physiology on trading floors have identified – so physically fit traders are more likely than unfit traders to optimise their trading abilities;
- Trading is physiological – George Soros, for example, is wise to regard backaches as a sign to trade (backaches are a classic sign of adrenal fatigue and high cortisol levels). The ability to trust physiological instincts is just one factor that sets Soros apart from others but can be learnt as a skill by everyone;
- Strength training – as well as cardiovascular training – is crucial in reversing the negative variables that cause emotional, irrational trading to occur;
- Sleep and a great diet, including supplementation (e.g. magnesium, Omega oils), are crucial in lowering cortisol levels. Massage, mindfulness, stretching and regular exposure to nature also offer highly effective routes to lowering stress levels;
- The right music enjoyed a commute to and from work can help significantly in optimising a trader or investor's emotional state. This subsequently exerts a positive effect on their ability to trade less emotionally (particularly in the morning when testosterone and cortisol levels are likely to be higher).

Special feature: maturity, mindfulness and the management of exuberance

Dermot Murphy is the Managing Director and Head of Global Loan and Special Situations Group at HSBC. In this special feature, Dermot shares his vast experience of trading in a pre- and post-crisis world, how traders are learning to better manage physiological stressors, why hiring more mature traders helps to manage exuberance and how close the Wall Street stereotype really is to the modern-day professional trader.

Q. *How accurate is the stereotypical Wall Street portrayal of excess in trading?*

Much of the concept and context of exuberance and excess in the trading sphere tends to come from the caricature of a trader derived from the Hollywood spectre of movies such as *The Wolf of Wall Street*, *Wall Street* and *Boiler Room*. This leadership scenario, where a specific personality type which embodies aggression in the pursuit of objectives with complete disregard for all controls and regulations, is largely mythical and exaggerated for cinematic effect.

Trading is ultimately the same as most other walks of life, where you have certain personality types that have been drawn towards dramatization of the process, and excesses of emotion. The desk reality is much less sensational or dramatic. Controls are much more evident post-2008 and a greater awareness of behaviour patterns distinguishing acceptable from unacceptable. Equally, emphasis is given to evaluation of contagion across assets and markets, and controlling the risk of bubbles or excesses and overheating in markets.

Traders can be drawn by myopia or cognitive bias towards a certain risk approach, and sometimes bias is amplified by market activity. Much of the controls and regulation strive to mitigate and inhibit the associated risks. In general most experienced traders will constantly rationalise, and re-evaluate, their trading thesis, to mitigate any unexplained bias in their approach.

Q. *Have the exuberances that caused the 2008 financial crisis been reined in?*

Through 1980s–early 2000s, many trading careers resembled that of a professional sports athlete, in that it was more intensive and spanned a shorter period of time.

The 2008 watershed, which focused on the Lehman Brothers insolvency, amplified stress and distress levels at individual and institutional levels. The mood and mind-set across trading floors were perplexed as such an occurrence was without precedent and inexplicable at the time. This event and the subsequent reverberations has focused individual traders, institutional risk management and regulators on the correlation and systematic nature of risk. The concept of excesses and aggression that led to the build-up of risks in the system at that time were not due to the actions of individual traders, but of a collective risk consensus across an entire industry. At trader level, institutional level, and industry level, an aligned consensus on funding, risk and asset values magnified this risk. Many risk profiles and correlations were commoditised and normalised and consequently underestimated.

Post 2008 there has been a conscious and sustained effort to adjust behaviour and process through controls, education, risk awareness/management and regulation. The industry has changed whereby certain personality types, behaviour patterns and certain profiles tended to dominate the agenda and consequently the templates for success were certain high profile, high-intensity, high risk personalities, more characteristic of the stereotype. Formerly, animated vocal energy were seen as being very important – you had to bring a lot of urgency and immediacy to proceedings. Now, to sustain a trading career requires a focus that can be maintained at an engaged level for a longer period of time, and traders have really removed extremes from the picture in order to do that.

Trader performance is currently measured more holistically. The short term performance reward structure has been aligned to incentivise longer term, consistent performance.

Q. Are there any safety mechanisms built in to the trading environment to guard against emotional trading?

There is much greater risk awareness and an increased number of controls at the individual, institutional and regulatory levels, currently embedded within the trading framework and process. Post-2008 crisis, a lot of the regulatory aspects have built in controls for traders in the way they approach trades.

The increasing electronification of elements of the trading process, has led to a relatively consistent and relentless period of changing dynamics across trading floors.

While there is a lot of energy on the trading floor, there are different dynamics and controls that establish more patience in how people engage. In trading, controls that increase awareness and identification of negative behaviours patterns are helpful. There is currently greater emphasis on the fairness and quality of content than the quantity of business.

The capacity for emotional and exuberant trading activity seems controlled, while maintaining a lot of energy in the industry. The regulatory and controls process has extended much further towards the individual rather than the institution.

Q.   Are excesses and exuberance still a feature of trading?

There are always going to be anecdotal stories of excess and addiction in trading – although I have rarely come across it in my own experience. I think that as the age profile has changed dramatically, as it has in recent years, the industry has matured, people have become more conscious of the concept of excess, and there is less extreme behaviour. That's not to say it doesn't exist, but the demonstration of it is a lot less evident than I think the mainstream stereotype would have you believe.

I also think the traders are now more aware of behavioural traits that could lead to concern and, whilst the situation is still not perfect, there is a big difference between the culture of 2006–8 and today. Generally, there is now a lot more maturity in the process of trading, far more regulatory controls, and, consequently, probably less risk. There is also more surveillance and probably a lot more knowledge on both the institution and trader side that ultimately help traders make more considered, rational decisions.

Q.   Research indicates that hiring more mature traders might lead to less exuberance and excess. Do you agree?

I attribute some of positive changes in the industry to the increasing age profile and experience set across the trading floor, and an industry which has greater maturity, less intense energy, a more durable, extendable career profile. There is also a material change in the trading floor culture. For example, what I have found with most traders that I work with now is that there is an energy level that can sometimes spill into stress, but these days, the actual intensity level on the trading floor – the frustration and anxiety typically displayed by traders and sales people has reduced meaningfully. What also seems to be different is that, pre-2008, success was governed largely results oriented, whereas now the emphasis is more balanced on process, suitable counterparts, risk and outcome and the fairness of that outcome.

The average age profile of bank trading floors has changed from a young population with a high turnover to a greater maturity profile which is a lot more balanced right across the age spectrum. This allows a lot more of a gradual progression throughout a trading career, and I think that this helps counterbalance excesses and exuberance while maintaining very positive energy. Greater longevity of career can mitigate the myopic stereotype trader.

Q. Are bubbles and crashes an inevitability of human nature?

All finance professionals are conscious of identifying bubbles and market overheating and the aftermath of 2008 financial crises highlights the consequent painful correction process. The build-up phase of financial bubble, tulip or real estate bubbles are typical of a loss of objectivity, and awareness of the risks comes too late to adjust risk or behaviour sufficiently.

Hindsight is a great perspective from which to comment, and I like to think that bubbles on the scale of the 2008 crisis are not inevitable but can be managed and the consequence on the broader economy mitigated. Human behaviour beyond the world of finance and trading, has a capacity for excess. Many forms of unchallenged consensus can create unanticipated risk, and is a broader psychological consideration that traders can learn from.

Q. Traders often experience cortisol over-production as a result of their constant exposure to the unpredictability of the financial markets. How might these risks be mitigated?

Everybody experiences tense situations in their careers and occupations, and many people can derive energy from these situations or undergo substantial stress and anxiety as a consequence. As a trader I think a lot comes down to an individual's reaction to a stress event, in terms of a) what the event is and b) what his/her response capacity to that event is. Traders similar to other occupations will achieve greater results with the appropriate infrastructure/ support and controls around them. It is very difficult and unrewarding to be under a constant state of heightened stress in any occupation. If trading, managing risk and making the associated decisions create heightened anxiety and continuous stress there are likely possibly alternative careers in the industry which are more suitable. Similar to a penalty shoot-out in football, not every player rushes to take a penalty, but clearly some players thrive on the opportunity, but both player-types are critical to the team performance in different ways.

Trading has a greater capacity for scenarios or individuals to create stressful episodes than may other occupations. Many of the controls, infrastructure, and personal techniques are all helpful to manage the emotions in constructive process and output. Many traders engage mindfulness, yoga, exercise, balance, and lifestyle to maintain a better perspective. And maybe it's my own age profile, but I think mindfulness, and taking time out, to contemplate, and avoid being rushed in to a decision, is a more accepted concept. I think any stigma for seeking help if needed has reduced, and banks actively encourage traders to use healthcare facilities and support services.

Reaction to stress, emotional trading and behaviour have been supported by the development of effective controls, awareness, support and experience. There is less spontaneity in trading than would have been evident previously, and much greater awareness around the psychology and physiology of the process.

Special feature: anabolic arbitrage

In this Special Feature, I spoke to 4-time British and WNBF World Champion pro natural bodybuilder, coach and Natural Muscle Editor (www.naturalmuscle.co.uk) Jon Harris, who shares his insights into why fitness training creates champions – in bodybuilding, trading and life.

Testosterone plays a vital role in bodybuilding as it's the main anabolic hormone responsible for increasing strength and building lean muscle tissue. Weight training stimulates it further still, and this is good news for recovery and accelerating gains, but it can lead to increased anger and aggression too. Bodybuilders take out their aggression on the weights – it's an integral part of the sport – which invariably leads to a great workout, so it's a win–win. But in trading there is no outlet. I'm not surprised that aggressive trades, for example, happen more often than they should.

As with sport, successful traders are in part selected for their high testosterone – translating into strength, confidence, willingness to take risks, and so on. However, without a physical outlet for the effects of testosterone it's dangerous. You'll harbour aggression, which of course is bad news if you happen to be working in a high-pressure environment with no release valve to press – which is exactly what traders face, so it comes out in bad trades. This is the reason why I always tell people in stressful office jobs to get plenty of exercise outside work.

Cortisol is another big problem. Too much can suppress your immune system and hamper recovery, and the harder and longer you train in a gym – or trade in a bank – the more this hormone is produced. This creates a limit for how much exercise you can do before the effects of excess cortisol become overbearing. To complicate matters, non-physical stress can also trigger its release, such as worry, anger, or a lack of sleep. Bodybuilders consciously manage cortisol by building in rest periods to avoid over-training, by developing good sleeping habits and by avoiding too many outside stressors – or by developing strategies to cope with stress better. This is exactly what traders need to find a way to do else cortisol over-production is inevitable.

Q. Why is it so crucial to be able to manage your emotions effectively?

The combination of restricted calories and hard, intense training can be really harsh for competitive bodybuilders, leading to tiredness, lack of energy, food cravings, waves of low mood and skewed thinking. This can make competition training difficult, or even force a competitor to give up. Over time I've learned to notice the signs and take a step back when needed. Traders are going to see some of these same signs and they need to develop the physiological self-awareness to know when to step back too, else trading addictions, burnout, etc., are going to be a real risk.

You need to develop the ability to keep a fairly level head when posed with a stressful situation that could trigger an emotional response or an irrational decision. You also need to develop the ability to not live in fear of making mistakes. They're part of what makes us human, and have evolved for good reasons. Shutting the door on negative emotions only makes things worse in my experience, so you might as well find a strategy to work with them.

I feel those emotions, particularly fear, quite strongly actually. In my own case, I try to not to block them, but rather see them for what they are, isolate them and try to just quietly observe them. I feel ultimately that the path to success in anything is never linear or straightforward. I've always believed that you need to develop a healthy relationship with failure, and use it as learning tool rather than a reason to not try something or quit. Having a reasonable baseline of confidence and self-assuredness does help with handling failure, which admittedly is not always easy to achieve and maintain, but it should be something to aspire to. One way to develop this is empowering yourself with knowledge – about the physiology of what makes you succeed or fail, about a deeper knowledge of what makes the markets tick. . .

Q. Rest is a vital part of your sport – and for traders. Why?

Growth and recovery really only occurs during rest. For a body-builder, if you don't allow sufficient rest between workouts, then the growth stage can't complete and you'll either slow your progress, halt it, or in the worst case even start regressing (over-training). The symptoms are easy to spot and include fatigue, tiredness, lack of appetite and a reduced capacity and desire to train. When resting, the body also repairs itself – and the brain does too – so bodybuilders tend to augment their training with lots of rest, and the foundation here is always a good night's sleep. Traders need rest just as crucially – the brain chemistry is the same.

If you interrupt the rest cycle, you'll inevitably be short-circuiting. It's worth noting that GH (growth hormone – a powerful peptide hormone that's key to recovery) is released during sleep, and so any attempt to reduce or manipulate your sleep patterns can adversely affect GH release and therefore further hamper the body's capacity to repair. Since a lack of sleep or rest also raises cortisol levels, this too will pull the brakes even harder on recovery for a trader or an athlete, leading to sub-par performance. Lifting weights can increase GH – just one of the many benefits of our sport.

Q.   *On the universal benefits of strength training: it's not sport, but fitness training, that the world of business can benefit from.*

I'm not surprised that science shows strength training to be crucial in stress management. I'd say that I've always gotten at least as much mental benefit from training with weights as I have with cardio. It's helped me from the perspective of reducing stress levels at work and increasing my powers of concentration, quite aside from all the physical benefits of sculpting your physique and improving your body image. I've spoken with successful people in business who seem in pretty poor shape – overweight, over-stressed and sleep deprived with all the alarm bells ringing. I wonder how much happier and ultimately successful they would be if they really looked after themselves both physically and mentally.

Whatever your line of work, you will always benefit from cultivating a balanced hormonal environment that promotes clear thinking and minimises emotional triggers. Without being a finance expert I can certainly see how traders are liable to make emotional decisions when faced with having to process large amounts of information quickly and make risky decisions – so I'd say they're a prime candidate to benefit here from a healthier way of life.

Q.   *On rolling the dice one last time for a final shot at the World Championship.*

It was 2006, and I can recall agonising really hard over whether to contest the World Championships in New York that year, which was only three months away at the time. I couldn't delay the decision any longer. I took myself off for a long walk to clear my head. Sat on a gate and watching the sunset, I put it to myself, 'Jon – you can do three things: you can either walk away, you can try and fail, or you can try and succeed'. With two runner-up spots behind me I realised this would likely be my third and last attempt. I contemplated the decision for a while, then took a deep breath and made the commitment to roll the dice one more time and see what I could really do if I put my mind to it.

I needed to make up ground fast and was up to six days a week training in no time. Factor in between one and two hours of cardio a day, and there's not much time for anything else. I was living and breathing this thing. My bodyweight held tight but due to the high output I was able to build muscle and burn fat simultaneously and could see my body changing almost daily. The last couple of weeks were horrendous. Energy levels were so low it felt like I was surviving on fresh air. I was moody and irritable, but my physique was holding up great.

Twelve weeks later after the most gruelling prep I'd ever completed, I stood onstage in NYC in the best shape of my life, waiting for the final announcement. Hearing my name in first place was surreal. Three months of hell, and years of effort before that flashed before my eyes. The middleweight gold medal was finally mine, and moments later I had defeated the lightweight and heavyweight champions to claim the overall world title. It was a truly humbling experience and a major life goal was achieved, but I have to remind myself that I very nearly didn't do that show at all. It taught me that the margin between achieving success and failure can be small, so don't stop until you're over the finish line.

Notes

1 Summary of studies discussed by B. J. Richards (2013), *Acetyl-L-Carnitine delivers fast anti-depressant benefits*, accessed at: www.wellnessresources.com/health/articles/acetyl-l-carnitine_delivers_fast_anti-depressant_benefits/

2 The author, Dr. Elesa Zehndorfer, is a 3-time British Championships finalist and class winner in natural bodybuilding and uses this exact approach to achieve a maximally lean condition.

Glossary

Adrenal glands: These glands produce a range of hormones including adrenaline and cortisol.

Adrenaline: Adrenaline is a hormone that is secreted by the adrenal gland in response to physical or mental stress (e.g. fear, panic). It is regulated by the autonomic nervous system and causes an increase in blood pressure, respiratory rate (breathing rate) and heart rate. It is also known as epinephrine.

Allele: Different versions of the same gene are known as 'alleles' – e.g. the serotonin L or S allele discussed primarily in Chapter 3. The 'long' and 'short' in the chapter title is actually a play on words, relating to serotonin L and S alleles.

Allostatic load: The physiological result of chronic and repeated stress on the body, caused primarily by repeated cortisol and adrenaline over-production.

Arbitrage: Arbitrage allows a trader to profit from differences in price in identical assets across different markets.

Bonds: A bond is a type of IOU that is issued by a government, local authority or company as a means of raising capital.

Buy-and-hold strategy: A buy-and-hold strategy is a passive investment strategy that involves buying stocks and holding them for a long period of time, ignoring short term fluctuations in value to realise longer-term profit.

Contrarian investing: Contrarian investing requires deep, fundamental analysis to identify investing opportunities that the wider market has missed as a result of hubris, sentiment and insufficient analysis. Contrarians take advantage of exploitable mis-pricings in securities markets.

Cortisol: The 'stress hormone', produced by the adrenal glands in response to stress.

Day trading: Day trading is the act of buying and selling a stock within the same day. Day traders take advantage of small price movements in highly liquid stocks or indexes to generate a profit. Some day traders can trade up to hundreds of times a day (e.g. scalpers).

Derivative: A derivative is a collective term used to describe a wide range of financial instruments whose price derives from, or depends, on the performance of other underlying investments.

DHEA: DHEA, otherwise known as dehydroepiandrosterone, is the most abundant hormone in our bodies and is produced by the adrenal glands and in the brain. It enables the production of androgens (such as testosterone and cortisol) and oestrogens and is anabolic, involved in cell regeneration and repair. DHEA levels generally begin to decline after the age of 30.

Distressed debt: Distressed debt refers to the debt owed by companies that have filed for bankruptcy, are likely to declare bankruptcy or are likely to enter another form of restructuring in the near future.

Dopamine: Dopamine is a catecholamine (a class of molecules that serve as both neurotransmitters and hormones) and a precursor of adrenaline. It is known as a 'happy' or 'reward' chemical and has been linked to pleasurable sensations when we anticipate or experience something pleasurable, and in the use of drugs, stimulants, trading, gambling and other sensation-seeking pursuits.

Endorphins: A chemical that is naturally released into the brain to reduce feelings of pain and enervate the body's opioid receptors, leading to a 'natural high'.

Exchange-traded fund (ETF):   An exchange-traded fund (ETF) is an equity-based product. It combines the characteristics of an individual share with those of a collective fund.

GABA: GABA (gamma-aminobutyric acid) is an amino acid which provides the main inhibitory (calming) neurotransmitter in the brain and plays a vital role in muscle-building. It is often used in treatments for stress disorders.

Growth hormone: Growth hormone, also known as somatotropin, promotes cell regeneration and growth and is therefore an anabolic. It plays a crucial role in emotional and cognitive well-being and can be increased by deep, high quality sleep and strength training.

Hedge: Hedging, which is where the name 'hedge fund' comes from, involves protecting investments against investment risk by strategically utilising one financial instrument to offset the risk of losing money as a result of negative price movements by another negatively correlated instrument.

Hedonism: The study of pleasure and pain and its defining role in human motivation and action.

Investor: An investor generally takes a longer-term view than a trader and invests capital with the aim of generating a long-term return, e.g. some hedge funds lock in an investor's capital for five years with the aim of utilising profitable buy-and-hold strategies and value investing strategies to generate profits.

Junk bonds: Junk bonds, also known as 'high yield' (high interest payable as a result of the riskiness of the asset), 'toxic', 'non-investment grade' or 'speculative' bonds, carry poor credit ratings, but are considered a good investment by some as they offer potentially high returns.

L-MAOA (also known as 'the warrior gene'): L-MAOA is a gene that plays a role in the expression of dopamine, norepinephrine and serotonin. Thought to predict behavioural aggression.

Limbic system: The limbic system, which includes the hippocampus and amygdala, is an area of the brain that manages instincts, mood and all basic emotions (e.g. fear, pleasure) and drives all pleasure-seeking activity (e.g. hunger, sexual urges, addictions).

Main Street (retail investors): A colloquial term used to describe non-institutional ('armchair') investors and traders.

Money laundering: Money laundering refers to the fraudulent act of attempting to convert the proceeds of criminal activity into legitimate money.

Neurogenesis: The creation of new brain tissue.

Neurotransmitters: A neurotransmitter is a substance (e.g. dopamine, acetylcholine, norepinephrine) that is released on excitation and excites or inhibits the target cell.

Oxytocin: Oxytocin is a hormone released by the pituitary gland and is known as the 'love hormone' as it stimulates behaviours responsible for sensations of love and bonding.

Physiology: Physiology is a branch of biology that deals with the functions and activities of life or of living matter (such as organs, tissues or cells) and of the physical and chemical phenomena involved. Sport physiology refers to the sub-discipline of physiology that focuses exclusively on the role of physiology on sports performance.

Ponzi scheme: A Ponzi scheme is a fraudulent scheme whereby the schemer creates a non-existent enterprise, advertising profitable investing returns to attract new investors, but in reality, using the investments of one investor to pay returns to another. The scheme is named after Charles Ponzi, the first man to use such a scheme. A recent famous example is former NASDAQ Chairman Bernard Madoff.

Prefrontal cortex: An area of the brain responsible for executive function (e.g. impulse control, reasoning, rational logic, goal setting and adherence, higher cognition, emotional control).

Serotonin: Formed from tryptophan (which can be derived from some foods, as a supplement or endogenously), serotonin acts as a neurotransmitter and effects control of pain, sleep and mood. It is often used as part of treatments for depression.

Steroids: Steroids can be exogenous (external to the body, e.g. anabolic steroid Winstrol) or endogenous (internal to the body, e.g. testosterone, cortisol) and is the name given to one of the chemical substances that are produced in the body.

Testosterone: Testosterone is a steroid hormone that is responsible for the development of male secondary sexual characteristics, and which plays a role in aggression, confidence and risk-taking.

Trader: A trader is an individual who buys and sells financial assets. There are different types of trader – e.g. day trader, momentum trader, scalper, position trader.

Value investing: A value investor (e.g. distressed debt investor) uses fundamental, technical analysis to identify stocks that the market has under- or over-valued, and seeks to generate a profit once the price of the stock goes up or down.

Volatility: Volatility refers to the fluctuations in the price of a security, commodity, currency or index and mathematically can be expressed as the square root of the standard deviation of an asset's return over a certain period. It is possible to trade volatility by trading future contracts or options (puts or calls) on future contracts on the VIX (the Chicago Board Options Exchange Volatility Index, which shows 30-day volatility constructed using the implied volatilities of a wide range of S&P 500 index options) or VIX-related ETFs.

Wall Street (institutional investors):   Institutions that invest funds on behalf of themselves and others, e.g. banks, insurance companies, pensions, hedge funds and mutual funds.

References

Akerlof, G. A. (2003). Behavioral macroeconomics and macroeconomic behavior. *The American Economist*, 47, 1, 25–47.

Aldrete, G. S., and Aldrete, A. (2012). *The Long Shadow of Antiquity: What Have the Greeks and Romans Done for Us?* A&C Black.

Anderson, A. (2008). *Is Online Trading Gambling with Peanuts?* SSRN eLibrary.

Andersson, A. M., Carlsen, E., Petersen, J. H., and Skakkebaek, N. E. (2003). Variation in levels of serum inhibin B, testosterone, estradiol, luteinizing hormone, follicle-stimulating hormone, and sex hormone-binding globulin in monthly samples from healthy men during a 17-month period: Possible effects of seasons. *The Journal of Clinical Endocrinology & Metabolism*, 88, 932–937.

Andruszliewicz, G., Davis, M., and Lleo, S. (2013). Taming animal spirits: Risk management with behavioural factors. *Annals of Finance*, 9, 145–166.

Anon. (2009). Want to reduce risk? Hire women, older men for trading floor. *Securities Industry News*.

Anon. (2016, September 16). Worried about cybercrime? Then consider the 'hack' ETF. *ETF News*. Accessed at: http://etfdailynews.com/2016/09/21/worried-about-cybercrime-then-buy-the-hack-etf/

Apicella, C. L., Dreber, A., Campbell, B., Graye, P. B., Hoffman, M., and Little, A. C. (2008). Testosterone and financial risk preferences. *Evolution and Human Behavior*, 29, 384–390.

Apicella, C. L., Dreber, A., and Mollerstrom, J. (2014). Salivary testosterone change following monetary wins and losses predict future financial risk-taking. *Psychoneuroendocrinology*, 39, 58–64.

Aron, A., Norman, C., Aron, E., McKenna, C., and Heyman, R. (2000). Couples' shared participation in novel and arousing activities and experienced relationship quality. *Journal of Personality and Social Psychology*, 78, 273–284.

Astell-Burt, T., Feng, X., and Kolt, G. S. (2013). Does access to neighbourhood green space promote a healthy duration of sleep? Novel findings from a cross-sectional study of 259319 Australians. *BMJ Open*, 3, 1–7.

Ayer, A. J. (1946). *Language, Truth & Logic*. New York: Dover Publications.

Baddeley, M. (2010, January 27). Herding, social influence and economic decision-making: Socio-psychological and neuroscientific analyses. *Philosophical Transactions of the Royal Society B: Biological Sciences*, 365, 1538, 281–290.

Baddeley, M. (2013). *Behavioural Economics and Finance*. London; New York: Routledge.

Baker, G. (2000). The use of performance measures in incentive contracting. *American Economic Review*, 90, 415–420.

Balchunas, Eric. (2016, March 7). The ETF files: How the U.S. government inadvertently launched a $3 trillion industry. *Bloomberg Markets*. Accessed at: www.bloomberg.com/features/2016-etf-files/?cmpid=yhoo.headline

Balchunas, Eric. (2017, February 6). U.S. ETFs 2017 outlook. *Bloomberg Intelligence*. Accessed at: www.bloomberg.com/professional/blog/u-s-etfs-2017-outlook/

Barber, B., and Odean, T. (2001). Boys will be boys: Gender, overconfidence, and common stock investment. *Quarterly Journal of Economics*, 116, 261–292.

Barber, B., and Odean, T. (2003). Trading is hazardous to your wealth: The common stock investment performance of individual investors. *The Journal of Finance*, LV, s. 773–806.

Barberis, N., and Shleifer, A. (2003). Style investing. *Journal of Financial Economics*, 68, 2, 161–199.

Barberis, N., and Thaler, R. (2002). *A survey of behavioural finance*. Working Paper No. 9222. National Bureau of Economic Research, Cambridge, MA.

Barberis, N., and Xiong, W. (2008, October). Realization utility. NBER Working Paper No. w14440. Accessed at: https://ssrn.com/abstract=1289674

Barnea, A., Cronqvist, H., and Siegel, S. (2010). Nature of nurture: What determines investor behaviour? *Journal of Financial Economics*, 98, 583–604.

Barrett, C. (2015, December 18). Ups and downs of a stock market rollercoaster year. *Financial Times*. Op Ed. Accessed at: https://www.ft.com/content/e161ba86-a4bd-11e5-97e1-a754d5d9538c

Bauer, C. C., Díaz, J., Concha, L., and Barrios, F. A. (2014). Sustained attention to spontaneous thumb sensations activates brain somatosensory and other proprioceptive areas. *Brain & Cognition*, 87, 86–96.

Bauer, I., Hughes, M., Rowsell, R., Cockerell, R., Pipingas, A., Crewther, S., and Crewther, D. (2014, March 29). Omega-3 supplementation improves cognition and modifies brain activation in young adults. *Human Psychopharmacology*, 2, 133–144. Accessed at: https://www.ncbi.nlm.nih.gov/pubmed/24470182

Baupost Group, Inc., The. (1999, December 17). Baupost Investor Letter. Accessed at: http://www.sitkapacific.com/files/Seth-Klarman-Baupost-Group-Letters_1999-12.pdf

Belisheva, N. K., Popov, A. N., Petukhova, N. V., Pavolva, K. S., Osipov, K. S., Tkachenko, S. E., and Baranova, T. I. (1995). Qualitative and quantitative evaluation of the effect of geomagnetic field variations on the functional state of the human brain. *Biophysics*, 40, 5, 1007–1014.

Bénabou, R. (2013). Groupthink: Collective delusions in organizations and markets. *The Review of Economic Studies*, 80, 2, 429–462.

Bentham, J. (1823). *An Introduction to the Principles of Morals and Legislation*, Volume 1. Oxford: Clarendon Press.

Bharara, P. (2009, November 19). Address on White Collar Crime. Speech given at NYU Law School. Accessed at: http://www.law.nyu.edu/sites/default/files/ECM_PRO_063924.pdf

Bhattacharya, U., Loos, B., Meyer, S., and Hackethal, A. (2017). Abusing ETFs. *Review of Finance*, 21, 3, 1217–1250.

Black, D. W. (1986) Compulsive buying: A review. *Journal of Clinical Psychiatry*, 57, 50–55.

Blakeslee, S. (2003, June 17). Brain experts now follow the money. *New York Times*. Accessed at: http://www.nytimes.com/2003/06/17/science/brain-experts-now-follow-the-money.html

Blasco, N., Corredor, P., and Ferreruela, S. (2012). Does herding affect volatility? Implications for the Spanish stock market. *Quantitative Finance*, 12, 311–327.

Bloomberg. (2017, August 1). Tesla could run out of cash making the Model 3, hedge fund billionaire says. *Fortune* online. Accessed at: http://fortune.com/2017/08/01/david-einhorn-model-3-tesla-elon-musk/

Booij, L., Welfeld, K., Leyton, M., Dagher, A., Boileau, I., Sibon, I., Baker, G. B., Diksic, M., Soucy, J. P., Pruessner, J. C., Cawley-Fiset, E., Casey, K. F., and Benkelfat, C. (2016). Dopamine cross-sensitization between psychostimulant drugs and stress in healthy male volunteers. *Translational Psychiatry*, 6, 1–8.

Booth, F. W., Chakravarthy, M. V., and Spangenburg, E. E. (2002). Topical review: Exercise and gene expression: Physiological regulation of the human genome through physical activity. *Journal of Physiology*, 543, 2, 399–411.

Bos, P. A., Panksepp, J., Bluthe, R. M., and van Honk, J. (2012). Acute effects of steroid hormones and neuropeptides on human social-emotional behaviour: A review of single administration studies. *Frontiers in Neuroendocrinology*, 33, 1, 17–35.

Bose, S., Ladley, D., and Li, X. (2016). *The role of hormones in financial markets*. Downloaded at: www.le.ac.uk/economics/research/RePEc/lec/leecon/dp16-01.pdf?uol_r=d307e306

Bryant, J., and Miron, D. (2003). Excitation-transfer theory. In J. Bryant, D. Roskos-Ewoldsen, and J. Cantor (Eds.), *Communication and Emotion: Essays in Honor of Dolf Zillmann* (pp. 31–59). Mahwah, NJ: Erlbaum.

Brymer, E., Davids, K., and Mallabon, L. (2014). Understanding the psychological health and well-being benefits of physical activity in nature: An ecological dynamics analysis. *Ecopsychology*, 6, 3, 189–197.

Bupp, Phillip. (2016, December 20). The Dallas Cowboys have a new 'intimidation coach'. *The Comeback*. Accessed at: http://thecomeback.com/nfl/the-dallas-cowboys-have-a-new-intimidation-coach.html

Buffet, W. (2013). *The Warren Buffet Way*. John Wiley & Sons, Inc.

Burger, D. (2017, May 15). Cyber-attack sends online security ETF surging. *Bloomberg Markets*. Accessed at: www.bloomberg.com/news/articles/2017-05-15/cyber-attacks-sends-online-security-etf-surging-as-fireeye-gains

Butcher, Sarah. (2015, April 27). Morning coffee: 'I wake up 3 times a night to check the Bloomberg.' Top Goldman trader's hot career tip. *Efinancial Careers*. Accessed at: http://news.efinancialcareers.com/uk-en/243318/bloomberg-addiction/

Caldú, X., and Dreher, J. (2007). Hormonal and genetic influences on processing reward and social information. *Annals of the New York Academy of Sciences*, 1118, 43–73.

Camerer, C. (1995). Individual decision making. In J. Kagel and A. Roth (Eds.), *Handbook of Experimental Economics*. Princeton, NJ: Princeton University Press.

Camerer, C. F., Loewestein, G., and Prelec, D. (2005). Neuroeconomics: How neuroscience can inform economics. *Journal of Economic Literature*, 43, 9–64.

Carnap, R. (1938, 1981). Logical foundations of the unity of science. In O. Hanfling (Ed.), *Essential Readings in Logical Positivism* (pp. 112–119). Oxford: Basil Blackwell.

Carr, D. B., Bullen, B. A., Skrinar, G. S., Arnold, M. A., Rosenblatt, M., Beitins, I. Z., Martin, J. B., and McArthur, J. W. (1981). Physical conditioning facilitates the exercise-induced secretion of beta-endorphin and beta-lipotropin in women. *The New England Journal of Medicine*, 305, 10, 560–563.

Carré, J. M., and Putnam, S. K. (2010). Watching a previous victory. *Psychoneuroendocrinology*, 35, 475–479.

Carroll, D., Ring, C., Suter, M., and Willemsen, G. (2000, June). The effects of an oral multivitamin combination with calcium, magnesium, and zinc on psychological well-being in healthy young male volunteers: A double-blind placebo-controlled trial. *Psychopharmacology* (Berl), 50, 2, 220–225. Accessed at: https://www.ncbi.nlm.nih.gov/pubmed/10907676

Cell Press. (2007, October 22). Press release: Sleep-deprivation causes an emotional brain 'disconnect'. *EurekAlert!* Accessed at: www.eurekalert.org/pub_releases/2007-10/cp-sca101707.php

Charlton, A. (2016, August 24). Elon Musk's $670m tweet: Tesla shares rocket ahead of surprise announcement. *International Business News*. Accessed at: http://www.ibtimes.co.uk/elon-musks-670m-tweet-tesla-shares-rocket-ahead-surprise-announcement-1577655

Chen, B. T., Yau, H. J., Hatch, C., Kusumoto-Yoshida, I., Cho, S. L., Hopf, F. W., and Bonci A. (2013, April 18). Rescuing cocaine-induced prefrontal cortex hypoactivity prevents compulsive cocaine seeking. *Nature*, 496, 7445, 359–362.

Chen, M., Su, T., Chen, Y., Hsu, J., Huang, K., Change, W., Chen, T., and Bai, Y. (2013). Association between psychiatric disorders and iron deficiency anemia among children and adolescents: A nationwide population-based study. *BMC Psychiatry*, 13, 61, 1–8.

Clark, D. M. (1986). A cognitive approach to panic. *Behaviour Research and Therapy*, 24, 461–470.

Coates, J. (2012a, June 21). The anatomy of a huge trading loss. *Time*. Accessed at: http://ideas.time.com/2012/06/21/the-anatomy-of-a-huge-trading-loss/print/

Coates, J. (2012b, July 6). Banks should train traders like athletes. *Financial Times*. Op Ed. Accessed www.ft.com/cms/s/0/9540a99c-c694-11e1-963a-00144feabdc0.html#axzz3xs4cDKp5.

Coates, J. (2012c). *The Hour Between Dog and Wolf: Risk Taking, Gut Feelings, and the Biology of Boom and Bust*. London: Fourth Estate.

Coates, J. (2012d). *The Hour Between Dog and Wolf: Risk Taking, Gut Feelings, and the Biology of Boom and Bust*. New York: Penguin Press.

Coates, J. (2014, June 7). The biology of risk. *New York Times Review*. Op Ed. Accessed at: https://www.nytimes.com/2014/06/08/opinion/sunday/the-biology-of-risk.html.

Coates, J. M., and Herbert, J. (2008, April 22). Endogenous steroids and financial risk taking on a London trading floor. *Proceedings of the National Academy of Sciences*, 105, 16, 6167–6172.

Coates, J. M., Gurnell, M., and Rustichini, A. (2009). Second-to-fourth digit ratio predicts success among high-frequency financial traders. *PNAS*, 106, 2, 623–628.

Coates, J. M., Gurnell, M., and Sarnyhai, Z. (2010). From molecule to market: Steroid hormones and financial risk-taking. *Philosophical Transactions of the Royal Society B*, 365, 331–343.

Coates, J. M., and Page, L. (2009). A note of trader sharpe rations. *PLOS One*, 4, 11, e8036.

Comstock, Courtney. (2010, April 5). Greenspan, you're losing the argument against Michael Burry, stop digging and stop acting like a fool. *Business Insider*. Accessed at: www.businessinsider.com/greenspan-on-michael-burry-scion-capital-2010-4?IR=T

Corodimas, K., LeDoux, J., Gold, P., and Schulkin, J. (1994). Corticosterone potentiation of learned fear. *Annals of the New York Academy of Sciences*, 746, 392–393.

Cunningham, T. (2016, January 8). Markets stabilise after a rollercoaster start to 2016. *Telegraph*. Accessed at: http://www.telegraph.co.uk/finance/markets/ftse100/12088643/Markets-stabilise-after-rollercoaster-start-to-2016.html

Cymbalista, F. (2003, July). How Soros knows what he knows. Part 1: The belief in fallability. *Stocks, Futures and Options*, 2, 7.

Dabbs, J. R., and Dabbs, M. G. (2000). *Heroes, Rogues and Lovers: Testosterone and Behavior*. McGraw-Hill.

Dabbs Jr., J. M., and Mallinger, A. (1999). High testosterone levels predict low voice pitch among men. *Personality & Individual Differences*, 27, 4, 801–804.

Damato, K. (2016, September 30). Jack Bogle sounds off: 10 provocative new pronouncements from the legendary founder of Vanguard. *Time Money*. Accessed at: http://time.com/money/4514371/jack-bogle-vanguard-founder-bogleheads/

Daniel, J. Z., Cropley, M., and Fife-Shaw, C. (2006, August). The effect of exercise in reducing desire to smoke and cigarette withdrawal symptoms is not caused by distraction. *Addiction*, 101, 8, 1187–1192.

Daniel, K., Hirshleifer, D., and Subrahmanyam, A. (1998). Investor psychology and security market under- and over-reactions. *Journal of Finance*, 53, 1839–1885.

Daniel, K. D., Hirshleifer, D., and Subrahmanyam, A. (2001). Overconfidence, arbitrage, and equilibrium asset pricing. *The Journal of Finance*, 56, 921–965.

De Bondt, W., and Thaler, R. (1995). Does the stock market overreact? *Journal of Finance*, 40, 793–807.

De Kloet, E. R. (2000, September 29). Stress in the brain. *European Journal of Pharmacology*, 405, 1–3, 187–198.

De Martino, B., Kumaran, D., Seymour, B., and Dolan, R. J. (2006). Frames, biases, and rational decision-making in the human brain. *Science*, 313, 5787, 684–687 / 1–9 [online]. Accessed at: https://www.ncbi.nlm.nih.gov/pmc/articles/PMC2631940/pdf/ukmss-3681.pdf

De Moor, M. H. M., Beem, A. L., Stubbe, J. H., Boomsma, D. I., and De Geus, E. J. C. (2006). Regular exercise, anxiety, depression, and personality: A population based study. *Preventative Medicine*, 42, 273–279.

de Quervain, D. J., Fischbacher, U., Treyer, V., Schellhammer, M., Schnyder, U., Buck, A., and Fehr, E. (2004). The neural basis of altruistic punishment. *Science*, 305, 5688, 1254–8.

de Vries, J. D., van Hooff, M. L., Geurts, S. A., and Kompier, M. A. (2016, March 31). Exercise as an intervention to reduce study-related fatigue among university students: A two-arm parallel randomized controlled trial. *PLoS One*, 11, 3, e0152137.

Deans, E. (2011). Magnesium and the brain: The original chill pill. *Psychology Today*. Accessed at: https://www.psychologytoday.com/blog/evolutionary-psychiatry/201106/magnesium-and-the-brain-the-original-chill-pill

Dexter, E. G. (1899). Influence of the weather upon crime. *Popular Science Monthly*, 55. Accessed at: https://en.wikisource.org/wiki/Popular_Science_Monthly

Dichev, I., and Janes, T. (2001). *Lunar cycle effects in stock returns*. Accessed at: http://papers.ssrn.com/abstract=281665.

Dickerson, S. S., and Kemeny, M. E. (2004, May). Acute stressors and cortisol responses: A theoretical integration and synthesis of laboratory research. *Psychological Bulletin*, 130, 3, 355–91

Dishman, R. K. (1986). Mental health. In V. Seefeldt (Ed.), *Physical Activity and Wellbeing* (pp. 304–341). Reston, VA: American Alliance for Health, Physical Education, Recreation and Dance.

Dishman, R. K., Berthoud, H. R., Booth, F. W., Cotman, C. W., Edgerton, V. R., Fleshner, M. R., Gandevia, S. C., Gomez-Pinilla, F., Greenwood, B. N., Hillman, C. H., Kramer, A. F., Levin, B. E., Moran, T. H., Russo-Neustadt, A. A., Salamone, J. D., Van Hoomissen, J. D., Wade, C. E., York, D. A., and Zigmond, M. J. (2006). Neurobiology of exercise. *Obesity*, 14, 3, 345–356.

Dishman, R. K., and Sothmann, M. (n.d.). Exercise fuels the brain's stress buffers. *American Psychological Association*. Accessed at: http://www.apa.org/help center/exercise-stress.aspx.

DOJ. (2016, October 24). *Pastor and Wife Indicted for $1.2 Million Fraud Targeting Church Members*. The United States Attorney's Office. Eastern District of Virginia. Accessed at: https://www.justice.gov/usao-edva/pr/pastor-and-wife-indicted-12-million-fraud-targeting-church-members

Dorn, A. J., Dorn, D., and Sengmueller P. (2014). Trading as gambling. *Management Science*, 61, 10, 2376–2393.

Dorn, D., and Sengmueller, P. (2009). Trading as entertainment? *Management Science*, 55, 591–603.

Dorn, J. (2014, March 19). When trading becomes a ruinous gambling addiction. *The Fix*. Accessed at: https://www.thefix.com/content/are-you-trading-or-gambling

Drakopoulos, S. A. (1990). Two levels of hedonistic influence on microeconomic theory. *Scottish Journal of Political Economy*, 37, 360–379.

Dreber, A., Apicella, C. L., Eisenberg, D. T. A., Garcia, J. R., Zamore, R. S., Lum, J. K., and Campbell, B. (2009). The 7R polymorphism in the dopamine receptor D4 gene (DRD4) is associated with financial risk taking in men. *Evolution and Human Behavior*, 30, 85–92.

Dufty, A. M. (1989). Testosterone and survival: A cost of aggressiveness? *Hormones & Behavior*, 23, 2, 185–193.

Dunckley, V. V. L. (2015, May). Screentime is making kids moody, crazy and lazy. *Psychology Today Online*. Accessed at: https://www.psychologytoday.com/blog/mentalwealth/201103/wired-and-tired-electronics-and-sleep-disturbance-in-children

Dutton, D. G., and Aron, A. P. (1974). Some evidence for heightened sexual attraction under conditions of high anxiety. *Journal of Personality and Social Psychology*, 30, 510–517.

Egan, M. (2016, January 20). From horrible to just bad: Dow ends down 249 points. *CNN Money*. Accessed at: http://money.cnn.com/2016/01/20/investing/stocks-markets-dow-oil-china/index.html

Egner, T., and Raz, A. (2007). Cognitive control processes and hypnosis. In G. A. Jamieson (Ed.), *Hypnosis and Conscious States: The Cognitive Neuroscience Perspective* (pp. 29–50). New York: Oxford University Press.

Einhorn, D. (2017, May 3). *Greenlight capital re first quarter result*. Conference Call.

Eisenegger, C., Haushofer, J., and Fehr, E. (2011, June). The role of testosterone in social interaction. *Trends in Cognitive Sciences*, 15, 6, 263–271.

Eisold, K. (2010). Anger & exercise. *Psychology Today*. Accessed at: https://www.psychologytoday.com/blog/hidden-motives/201008/anger-and-exercise

Ellis, A. (1975, August 30–September 2). *The Biological Basis of Human Irrationality*. Paper presented at the Annual Meeting of the American Psychological Association, 83rd, Chicago, IL.

Elster, J. (1996). Emotions and economic theory. *Journal of Economic Literature*, 36, 47–74.

Emory University Health Studies Center. (2006). Emory study lights up the political brain. *Science Daily*. Accessed at: www.sciencedaily.com/releases/2006/01/060131092225.htm.

Financial Crisis Inquiry Commission. (2010, March 17). *Transcript of Financial Crisis Inquiry Commission. Interview of Charles O. Prince*. Accessed at: http://fcic-static.law.stanford.edu/cdn_media/fcic-docs/2010-03-17%20transcript%20of%20FCIC%20staff%20interview%20with%20Charles%20Prince,%20Citigroup.pdf

Finch, Gavin. (2017, February 8). Brexit to cost UK 30,000 finance jobs and £1.6tn of bank assets, think tank Bruegel says. *Independent*. Accessed at: www.independent.co.uk/news/business/news/brexit-cost-city-london-finance-jobs-30000bank-assets-price-16tn-a7568231.html

Flier, J. S., and Underhill, L. H. (1998). Protective and damaging effects of stress mediators. *The New England Journal of Medicine*, 338, 3, 171–179.

Fogel, S. M., Nader, R., Cote, K. A., and Smith, C. T. (2007) Sleep spindles and learning potential. *Behavioral Neuroscience*, 121, 1–10.

Fong, T. W. (2005). The vulnerable faces of pathological gambling. *Psychiatry* (Edgmont), 2, 4, 34–42.

French, K. R., and Poterba, J. M. (1991). Investor diversification and international equity markets. *American Economic Review*, 81, 2, 222–226.

Friedman, M. (1953). The case for flexible exchange rates. In *Essays in Positive Economics* (pp. 157–203). Chicago: University of Chicago Press.

Frydman, C., Camerer, C., Bossaerts, P., and Rangel, A. (2010). MAOA-L carriers are better at making optimal financial decisions under risk. *Proceedings of the Royal Society*, 1–7.

Furness, J. B., Kunze, W., and Clerc, N. (1999, November). The intestine as a sensory organ: Neural, endocrine, and immune responses. *American Journal of Physiology-Gastrointestinal and Live Physiology*, 277, 5 Pt 1., G922–8.

Furnham, A. (2006). Personality disorders and intelligence. *Journal of Individual Differences*, 27, 42–46.

Galbraith, J. K. (1954/1988). *The Great Crash, 1929*. Harcourt: Houghton Mifflin.

Garcia, A. J., III, Zanella, S., Koch, H., Doi, A., and Ramirez, J. M. (2011). Networks within networks: The neuronal control of breathing. *Progress in Brain Research*, 188, 31–50.

Garcia, D. (2012). *The kinks in financial journalism*. Working Paper, University of North Carolina.

Gassendi, P. (1972). *The Selected Works of Pierre Gassendi*. Edited and translated by Craig B. Brush. New York: Johnson Reprint Corporation.

Giese, J., Nelson, B., Tanaka, M., and Tasahev, N. (2013). *How could macroprudential policy affect financial system resilience and credit? Lessons from the literature*. Financial Stability Paper No. 21, May, Bank of England.

Giese, M., Unternaehrer, E., Brand, S., Calabrese, P., Holsboer-Trachsler, E., and Eckert, A. (2013). The interplay of stress and sleep impacts BDNF level. *PLoS ONE*, 8, 10, 1–6.

Gilovich, T., Griffin, D., and Kahneman, D. (2002). *Heuristics and Biases: The Psychology of Intuitive Judgment*. New York: Cambridge University Press.

GMI Ratings. (2013, January 3). Recommended reading on forensic accounting. *Business Insider*. Accessed at: http://www.businessinsider.com/recommended-reading-on-forensic-accounting-2013-1?IR=T

Goetz, S. M. M., Shattuck, K. S., Miller, R. M., Campbell, J. A., Lozoya, E., Weisfeld, G. E., and Carré, J. M. (2013). Social status moderates the relationship between facial structure and aggression. *Psychological Science*, 24, 11, 2329–2334.

Goetzmann, W. N., and Dhar, R. (2004). *Bubble investors: What were they thinking?* Working Paper, School of Management, Yale University, New Haven, CT.

Goldberg, H., and Lewis, R. T. (1978). *Money Madness: The Psychology of Saving, Spending, Loving and Hating Money*. New York: William Morrow and Co.

Goldstein, R. Z., Alia-Klein, N., Tomasi, D., Zhang, L., Cottone, L. A., Maloney, T., Telang, F., Caparelli, E. C., Chang, L., Ernst, T., Samaras, D., Squires, N. K., and Volkow, N. D.et al. (2007, January). Is decreased prefrontal cortical sensitivity to monetary reward associated with impaired motivation and self-control in cocaine addiction? *American Journal of Psychiatry*, 164, 1, 43–51.

Goldstein, R., and Volkow, N. (2002). Drug addiction and its underlying neurobiological basis: Neuroimaging evidence for the involvement of the frontal cortex. *American Journal of Psychiatry*, 159, 1642–1652.

Gore, Al., and Blood, D. (2009). Time is up for short-term thinking in capitalism. *Financial Times*. Accessed at: www.ft.com/content/1b1067b2-dacd-11de-933d-00144feabdc0?mhq5j=e1

Grahn, P., and Stigsdotter, U. A. (2003). Landscape planning and stress. *Urban Forestry & Urban Greening*, 2, 1, 1–18.

Graham, B. (1949). *The Intelligent Investor: The Classic Text on Value Investing*. New York: HarperCollins.

Graham, B., and Dodd, L. D. (2009). *Security Analysis*. (6th ed.). McGraw-Hill.

Grandjean, A. C. (1997, May). Diets of elite athletes: Has the discipline of sports nutrition made an impact? *Journal of Nutrition*, 127, 5 Suppl, 874S–877S.

Granero, R., Tárrega, S., Fernández-Aranda, F., Aymamí, N., Gómez-Peña, M., Custal, N., Orekhova, L., Savvidou, L. G., Menchón, J. M., and Jiménez-Murcia, S. (2012). Gambling on the stock market: an unexplored issue. *Comprehensive Psychiatry*, 53, 666–673.

Grinblatt, M., and Keloharju, M. (2009a). Sensation seeking, overconfidence and trading activity. *The Journal of Finance*, 64, 549–578.

Grinblatt, M., and Keloharju, M. (2009b). Sensation seeking, risk appraisal, and risky behaviour. *Personality & Individual Differences*, 14, 14–52.

Gruzelier, J. H. (2006). Frontal functions, connectivity and neural efficiency underpinning hypnosis and hypnotic susceptibility. *Contemp. Hypnosis*, 23, 15–32.

Gruzelier, J., Egner, T., and Vernon, D. (2006). Validating the efficacy of neurofeedback for optimising performance. *Progress in Brain Research*, 159, 421–431.

Gutnik, L. A., Hakimzada, A. F., Yoskowitz, N. A., and Pater, V. L. (2006). The role of emotion in decision-making: A cognitive neuroeconomics approach toward understanding sexual risk behaviour. *Journal of Biomedical Informatics*, 39, 720–736.

Gwartney, D. (2009). *The testosterone: Cortisol connection muscular development*. Accessed at: www.musculardevelopment.com/contests/ifbb-chicago-pro-am/12-md-articles/1583-the-testosteronecortisol-connection.html#.WSXOv2jyvIU

Haiken, Melanie. (2014, June 12). More than 10,000 suicides tied to economic crisis, study says. *Forbes*. Accessed at: www.forbes.com/sites/melaniehaiken/2014/06/12/more-than-10000-suicides-tied-to-economic-crisis-study-says/#1a4a0ec21cbb

Halberg, F., Cornélissen, G., Otsuka, K., Watanabe, Y., Katinas, G. S., Burioka, N., et al. (2000). International BIOCOS study group: Cross-spectrally coherent ~ 10.5- and 21-year biological and physical cycles, magnetic storms and myocardial infarctions. *Neuroendocrinology Letters*, 21, 233–258.

Hall, V. (2016, January 8). Canadian kayaker Mark de Jonge not feeling weight of golden expectations heading into Rio Olympics. *National Post*. Accessed at: http://nationalpost.com/sports/olympics/canadian-kayaker-mark-de-jonge-not-feeling-weight-of-golden-expectations-at-rio-olympics

Harford, T. (2017, March 11/12). The facts need a champion. *FT.com Magazine*. p. 18.

Hennessey, J., and Levine, S. (1979). Stress, arousal and the pituitary-adrenal system: A psychoendocrine hypothesis. *Progress in Psychobiology & Physiobiological Psychology*, 8, 133–178.

Hermans, E. J., Putman, P., Baas, J., Koppeschaar, H., and van Honk, J. (2006). A single administration of testosterone reduces fear-potentiated startle in humans. *Biological Psychiatry*, 59, 872–874.

Higgins, S. T., Wong, C. J., Badger, G. J., Ogden, D. E., and Dantona, R. L. (2000). Contingent reinforcement increases cocaine abstinence during outpatient treatment and 1 year of follow-up. *Journal of Consulting Clinical Psychology*, 68, 64–72.

Hillman, C. H., Erickson, K. I., and Kramer, A. F. (2008, January). Be smart, exercise your heart: Exercise effects on brain and cognition. *Nature Reviews Neuroscience*, 9, 58–65.

Hirshleifer, D., and Shumway, T. (2003). *Good day sunshine: Stock returns and the weather*. Working Paper. University of Michigan Business School, Ann Arbor, MI.

Hulbert, Mark. (2017, February 1). The dangerous side of ETFs. *USA Today*. Accessed at: www.usatoday.com/story/money/columnist/2017/02/01/dangerous-side-etfs/97308332/

Isbitts, R. (2017, February 13). Will the stock market eat itself? *Forbes online*. Accessed at: https://www.forbes.com/sites/robisbitts2/2017/02/13/will-the-stock-market-eat-itself/#1460bfc64958

Jevons, W. S. (1888). *The Theory of Political Economy*. London: Macmillan & Co.

Jia, Y. (2014, May 23) Testosterone and Financial Misreporting. *Melbourne Accounting Research Seminars*. Accessed at: http://fbe.unimelb.edu.au/__data/assets/pdf_file/0003/1026678/MARS_Seminar_Yuping_Jia_23May2014.pdf

Jia, Y., Lent, L. V., and Zeng, Y. (2014). Masculinity, testosterone, and financial misreporting. *Journal of Accounting Research*, 52, 1195–1246.

Jones, D. N., and Paulhus, D. L. (2011). The role of impulsivity in the Dark Triad of personality. *Personality and Individual Differences*, 52, 679–682.

Jones, G. (2002). What is this thing called mental toughness? An investigation of elite sport performers. *Journal of Applied Sport Psychology*, 14, 3, 205–218.

Jorion, P. (2006, April). Keeping up with the Joneses: The desire of the desire for money. *Behavioral and Brain Sciences*, 29, 2, 187–188.

Joyner, M. J., and Coyle, E. F. (2007, January 1). Endurance exercise performance: The physiology of champions. *Journal of Physiology*, 586, Pt 1, 35–44.

Kademian, S., Bignante, A., Lardone, P., McEwen, B., and Volosin, M. (2005). Biphasic effects of adrenal steroids on learned helpnessness behaviour induced by indescapable shock. *Neuropsychopharm*, 30, 58–66.

Kahneman, D., Slovic, P., and Tversky, A. (1982). *Judgment Under Uncertainty: Heuristics and Biases*. Cambridge: Cambridge University Press.

Kahneman, D., and Tversky, A. (Eds.). (2000). *Choices, Values and Frames*. New York: Cambridge University Press.

Kamstra, M. J., Kramer, L. A., and Levi, M. D. (2003). Winter blues: Seasonal Affective Disorder (SAD) and stock market returns. *American Economic Review*, 93, 1, 324–343.

Kaplan, R. S., and Norton, D. (1992, January–February). The balanced scorecard: Measures that drive performance. *Harvard Business Review*, 70, 1, 71–79. (Reprint #92105.)

Kashkin, H. B., and Kleber, H. D. (1989, December 8). Hooked on hormones? An anabolic steroid addiction hypothesis. *JABA*, 262, 22, 3166–70.

Kennedy, M., and Agencies. (2013, November Friday 22). Bank intern Moritz Erdhardt died from epileptic seizure, inquest told. *Guardian*. Accessed at: www.theguardian.com/business/2013/nov/22/moritz-erhardt-merrill-lynch-intern-dead-inquest

Kenning, P., and Plassman, H. (2005). Neuro economics: An overview from an economic perspective. *Brain Research Bulletin*, 67, 343–354.

Kets de Vries, M. E. R. (2004). A clinical perspective on organizational dynamics. *European Management Journal*, 22, 183–200.

Keynes, J. M. (1936a). *The General Theory of Employment, Interest and Money*. New York: Harcourt, Brace and Company.

Keynes, J. M. (1936b). *The General Theory of Employment, Interest and Money*. London: Palgrave Macmillan.

Keynes, J. M. (1937). The general theory of employment. *Quarterly Journal of Economics*, 51, 209–223.

Keynes, J. M. (Ed.). (2007). *The General Theory of Employment, Interest and Money*. London: Palgrave Macmillan.

Kilpatrick, A. (1992). *Warren Buffett: the good guy of Wall Street*. Dutton.

Kindleberger, C. P., and Aliber, R. Z. (2005). *Manias, Panics and Crashes: A History of Financial Crises* (5th ed.). London: Palgrave Macmillan.

Klarman, S. A. (1991). *Margin of Safety: Risk-Averse Value Investing Strategies for the Thoughtful Investor*. Harper-Collins.

Klarman, S. (2017, February 7). *2016 Year-end letter*. The Baupost Group, LLC.

Kluger, J. (2013, May 3). The evil brain: What lurks inside a killer's mind. *Time*. Accessed at: http://science.time.com/2013/05/03/evil-brain/

Knutson, B., and Bossearts, P. (2007, August). Neural antecedents of financial decisions. *Journal of Neuroscience*, 27, 31, 8174–8177.

Knutson, B., Wimmer, G. F., Kuhnen, C. M., and Winkielman, P. (2008). Nucleus accumbens activation mediates the influence of reward cues on financial risk-taking. *NeuroReport*, 19, 509–513.

Kobasa, S. C., Maddi, S. R., Puccetti, M. C., and Zola, M. A. (1985). Effectiveness of hardiness, exercise, and social support as resources against illness. *Journal of Psychosomatic Research*, 29, 525–533.

Koelsch, S. (2010). Towards a neural basis of music-evoked emotions. *Trends in Cognitive Science*, 14, 3, 131–137.

Kolanovic, M., and Kaplan, B. (2017, October 3). What will the next crisis look like? *Mauldin Economics*. Accessed at: http://www.mauldineconomics.com/outsidethebox/what-will-the-next-crisis-look-like

Kolhatkar, S. (2013, September 12). Former Lehman CFO Erin Callan's never going back. *Bloomberg*. Accessed at: www.businessweek.com/articles/2013-09-12/former-lehman-cfo-erin-callans-never-going-back

Korpela, K., Borodulin, K., Neuvonen, M., Paronen, O., and Tyrväinen, L. (2014). Analyzing the mediators between nature-based outdoor recreation and emotional well-being. *Journal of Environmental Psychology*, 37, 1–7.

Krasnova, H., Wenninger, H., Widjaja, T., and Buxmann, P. (2013, February 27–March 1). Envy on Facebook: A hidden threat to users' life satisfaction? 11th International Conference on Wirtschaftsinformatik. Accessed at: www.ara.cat/2013/01/28/855594433.pdf?hash=b775840d43f9f93b7a9031449f809c388f342291

Krivelyova, A., and Robotti, C. (2003). *Playing the field: Geomagnetic storms and international stock markets*. Working Paper No. 2003–5a. Federal Reserve Bank of Atlanta.

Kroll, J. (2007). New directions in the conceptualization of psychotic disorders. *Current Opinion in Psychiatry*, 20, 573–7.

Kruger, J., and Dunning, D. (1999). Unskilled and unaware of it: How difficulties in recognizing one's own incompetence leads to inflated self-assessments. *Journal of Personality and Social Psychology*, 77, 6, 1121–1134.

Kuhnen, C. M., and Knutson, B. (2005). The neural basis of financial risk-taking. *Neuron*, 47, 763–770.

Kuo, F. E., and Sullivan, W. C. (2001). Environment and crime in the inner city: Does vegetation reduce crime? *Environment and Behavior*, 33, 3, 343–367.

Lambert, K. G. (2006). Rising rates of depression in today's society: Consideration of the roles of effort-based rewards and enhanced resilience in day-to-day functioning. *Neuroscience & Biobehavioral Review*, 30, 497–510.

LaPerriere, A., Antoni, M. H., Schneiderman, N., Ironson, G., Klimas, N., Caralis, P., and Fletcher, M. A. (1990). Exercise intervention attenuates emotional distress and natural killer cell decrements following notification of positive serologic status of HIV-1. *Biofeedback and Self-Regulation*, 15, 229–242.

Lattman, Peter. (2013, June 3). A tale of Wall St. excess. *DealB%k*. Accessed at: https://dealbook.nytimes.com/2013/06/03/a-tale-of-wall-st-excess/?_r=0

Laumann, K., Garling, T., and Stormark, K. M. (2003). Selective attention and heart rate responses to natural and urban environments. *Journal of Environmental Psychology*, 23, 125–134.

Lawrence Smith, E. (1939) *Tides in the Affairs of Men* (pp. x, 178). New York: The Macmillan Co.

Lea, S. E. G., and Webley, P. (2006). Money as tool, money as drug: The biological psychology of a strong incentive. *Behavioral and Brain Sciences*, 29, 161–209.

Lee, C. M. C., Shleifer, A., and Thaler, R. H. (1991). Investor sentiment and the closed-end fund puzzle. *Journal of Finance*, 46, 1, 75–109.

Lefevre, C. E., Lewis, G. J., Perrett, D. I., and Penke, L. (2013). Telling facial metrics: Facial width is associated with testosterone levels in men. *Evolution & Human Behavior*, 34, 273–279.

Leproult, R., and Van Cauter, E. (2011). Effect of 1 week of sleep restriction on testosterone levels in young healthy men. *JAMA: The Journal of the American Medical Association*, 305, 21, 2173.

Leproult., R., Copinschi., G., Buxton, O., and Van Cauter, E. (1997). Sleep loss results in an elevation of cortisol levels the next evening. *Sleep*, 20, 10, 865–870.

Lerner, R. M. (2009). The positive youth development perspective: Theoretical and empirical bases of a strength-based approach to adolescent development. In C. R. Snyder and S. J. Lopez (Eds.), *Oxford Handbook of Positive Psychology* (2nd ed., pp. 149–163). Oxford: Oxford University Press.

Levine, Matt. (2016, November 16). Hedge-fund losses and boutique hires. *Bloomberg*. Accessed at: www.bloomberg.com/view/articles/2016-11-16/hedge-fund-losses-and-boutique-hires

Lewandowski, G. W. Jr., and Aron, A. (2004). Distinguishing arousal from novelty and challenge in initial romantic attraction between strangers. *Social Behavior and Personality*, 32, 4, 361–372.

Lewis, G. J., Lefevre, C. E., and Bates, T. C. (2012). Facial width-to-height ratio predicts achievement drive in US presidents. *Personality and Individual Differences*, 52, 855–857.

Lewis, P. (2000, September). Realism, causation and the problem of social structure. *Journal for the Theory of Social Behaviour*, 30, 3, 249–268.

Linnet, J., Peterson, E., Doudet, D. J., Gjedde, A., and Møller, A. (2010). Dopamine release in ventral striatum of pathological gamblers losing money. *Acta Psychiatrica Scandinavica*, 122, 326–333.

Lo, A., and Repin, D. V. (2002). The psychophysiology of real-time financial risk processing. *Journal of Cognitive Neurosciences*, 14, 3, 323–339.

Loewenstein, G., Weber, E., and Hsee, C. (2001). Risk as feelings. *Psychological Bulletin*, 127, 267–286.

Logothetis, N. K. *What we can and what we can't do with fMRI*. Max Planck Institute for Biological Cybernetics Tübingen, Germany, and Imaging Science and Biomedical Engineering, University of Manchester, Manchester, UK. Accessed at: https://mail.google.com/mail/u/0/?tab=wm#search/dian/15b234a8aa8cdac6?projector=1.

Loomis, C.J. (2014, July 7). BlackRock: the $4.3trn force. *Fortune*. Accessed at: http://fortune.com/2014/07/07/blackrock-larry-fink/

Lord, James. (2017, March 9). ETF industry growth outstripping hedge funds, finds ETFGI. *ETF Strategy*. Accessed at: www.etfstrategy.co.uk/etf-industry-growth-outstripping-hedge-funds-finds-etfgi-37265/.

Lorenz, K. Z. (1963). *On Aggression*. London: Routledge.

Lowenstein, R. (2000). *When Genius Failed*. New York: Random House.

Lynch, D. J. (2016). Platinum partners charged in $1bn fraud. *FT Online*. Accessed at: www.ft.com/content/953518d2-c60a-11e6-8f29-9445cac8966f

Maddock, R. J., Garrett, A. S., and Buonocore, M. H. (2003). Posterior cingulate cortex activation by emotional words: FMRI evidence from a valence detection task. *Human Brain Mapping*, 18, 30–41.

Mäler, K. G., Aniyar, S., and Jansson A. (2008). Accounting for ecosystem services as a way to understand the requirements for sustainable development. *Proceedings of the National Academy of Sciences*, 105, 9501–9506.

Manesidis, G. (2013). *The function of hormones during the economic decision making process*. International Hellenic University. MSc Thesis.

Mansey, K., and Pancevski, B. (2013, August 25). City intern died on brink of top job. *The Times: The Sunday Times*. Accessed at: https://www.thetimes.co.uk/article/city-intern-died-on-brink-of-top-job-7c5st52n5mt

Markiewicz, L., and Weber, E. U. (2013). DOSPERT's gambling risk-taking propensity scale predicts excessive stock trading. *The Journal of Behavioural Finance*, 14, 65–78.

Marks, H. (2014, September 3). Memo to: Oaktree clients. Re: Revisiting Risk. Oaktree Capital Management LP. Accessed at: https://www.oaktreecapital.com/docs/default-source/memos/2014-09-03-risk-revisited.pdf?sfvrsn=2

Marsh, D., and Smith, M. (2001). Debates: There is more than one way to do political science: On different ways to study policy networks. *Political Studies*, 49, 3, 528–541.

Mazur, A., and Booth, A. (1998). Testosterone and dominance in men. *Behavioral and Brain Sciences*, 21, 353–363 discussion 363–397.

McEwen, B. S. (1998a). Protective and damaging effects of stress mediators. Seminars in medicine of the Beth Israel deaconess medical center. *The New England Journal of Medicine*, 338, 3, 171–179.

McEwen, B. (1998b). Stress, adaptation and disease: Allostasis and allostatic load. *Annals of the New York Academy of Sciences*, 840, 33–44.

McEwen, B. S. (2000). Allostasis and allostatic load: Implications for neuropsychopharmacology: Elsevier perspectives. *Neuropsychopharmacology*, 22, 2, 108–124.

McGonigal, K. (2011). Stress, sugar and self-control. *Psychology Today*. Accessed at: https://www.psychologytoday.com/blog/the-science-willpower/201111/stress-sugar-and-self-control

Mehta, P. H., and Josephs, R. A. (2006). Testosterone changes after losing predicts the decision to compete again. *Hormones and Behavior*, 50, 684–692.

Mehta, P. H., and Josephs, R. A. (2010). Testosterone and cortisol jointly regulate dominance: Evidence for a dual-hormone hypothesis. *Hormones & Behavior*, 58, 898–906.

Minsky, H. P. (1975). *John Maynard Keynes*. New York: Columbia University Press.

Mitterschiffthaler, M. T., Fu, C. H., Dalton, J. A., Andrew, C. M., and Williams, S. C. (2007). A functional MRI study of happy and sad affective states induced by classical music. *Human Brain Mapping*, 28, 10, 1150–1162.

Monaghan E. P., and Glickman S. E. (2001). Hormones and aggressive behavior. In J. B. Becker, S. M. Breedlove, and D. Crews (Eds.), *Behavioural Endocrinology* (pp. 261–287). Cambridge, MA: MIT Press.

Montague, P. R. (2007, October–December). Neuroeconomics: A view from neuroscience. *Functional Neurology*, 22, 4, 219–234.

Moore, K. S. (2013). A systematic review on the neural effects of music on emotion regulation: Implications for music therapy practice. *Journal of Music Therapy*, 50, 3, 198–242.

Morris, R. G. M. (2003). Long-term potentiation and memory. *Philosophical Transactions of the Royal Society of London B*, 358, 643–647.

Moskovic, D. J., Eisenberg, M. L., and Lipshultz, L. I. (2012, November–December). Seasonal fluctuations in testosterone-estrogen ratio in men from the Southwest united states. *Journal of Andrology*, 33, 6, 1298–1303.

Nuwer, R. (2014). Are you addicted to stress? Here's how to tell. *Huffington Post Online*. Accessed at: www.huffingtonpost.com/2014/08/19/stress-addiction_n_5689123.html.

Nuzzo, R. (2013, March 25). Brain scans predict which criminals are more likely to reoffend. *Nature News*. Accessed at: www.nature.com/news/brain/scans-predict-which-criminals-are-more-likely-to-reoffend-1.12672

O'Connor, P. J., Herring, M. P., and Caravalho, A. (2010). Mental health benefits of strength training in adults. *American Journal of Lifestyle Medicine*, 4, 5, 377–396.

Pacione, M. (2003). Urban environmental quality and human wellbeing – a social geographical perspective. *Landscape and Urban Planning*, 986, 1–12.

Palmer, J. A., Palmer, L. K., Michiels, K., and Thigpen, B. (1995). Effects of types of exercise on depression in recovering substance abusers. *Perceptual and Motor Skills*, 80, 523–530.

Panksepp, J. (1998). *Affective Neuroscience: The Foundations of Human and Animal Emotions*. New York: Oxford University Press.

Paris, J. J., Franco, C., Sodano, R., Frye, C. A., and Wulfert, E. (2010). Gambling pathology is associated with dampened cortisol response among men and women. *Physiology & Behavior*, 99, 230–233.

Park, A. (2012, January 9). Study: Stress shrinks the brain and lowers our ability to cope with adversity. *Time Magazine*. Health section.

Paul, E. F. (1979). *Moral Revolution and Economic Science*. Westport, CT: Greenwood Press.

Pavalko, R. (2001). *Problem Gambling and Its Treatment*. Springfield, IL: Charles, C Thomas Publisher, Ltd.

Payton, M. (2016, April 12). Sugar addiction should be treated as a form of drug abuse. *The Independent*. Accessed at: www.independent.co.uk/news/science/sugar-has-similar-effect-on-brain-as-cocaine-a6980336.html

Persinger, M. A. (1987). Geopsychology and geopsychopathology: Mental processes and disorders associated with geochemical and geophysical factors. *Experientia*, 43, 1, 92–104.

Peters, S., Stanley, I. M., Rose, M., Kaney, S., and Salmon, P. (2000). *A controlled study of group aerobic exercise in patients with persistent unexplained physical symptoms*. Unpublished report. University of Liverpool.

Peterson E., Moller A., Doudet D. J., Bailey C. J., Hansen K. V., Rodell A., et al. (2010). Pathological gambling: relation of skin conductance response to dopaminergic neurotransmission and sensation-seeking. *Eur. Neuropsychopharmacol.*, 20, 766–775.

Pfattheicher, S. (2016). Testosterone, cortisol and the Dark Triad: Narcissism (but not Machiavellianism or psychopathy) is positively related to basal testosterone and cortisol. *Personality and Individual Differences*, 97, 115–119.

Pfaus, J. G. (2009). Pathways of sexual desire. *The Journal of Sex Medicine*, 6, 1506–1533.

Popkin, B. M. (2006). Global nutrition dynamics: The world is shifting rapidly toward a diet linked with noncommunicable diseases. *American Journal of Clinical Nutrition*, 84, 289–298.

Pretty J. (2004). How nature contributes to mental and physical health. *Spirituality & Health Int*, 5, 2, 68–78.

Pretty, J., Griffin, M., Sellens, M., Pretty C., and Green, C. (2003). *Exercise: Complementary roles of nature, exercise and diet in physical and emotional well-being and implications for public health policy*. CES Occasional Paper 2003-1, University of Essex, Colchester.

Pretty, J., Peacock, J., Hine, R., Sellens, M., South, N., and Griffin, M. (2007). Green exercise in the UK countryside: Effects on health and psychological wellbeing, and implications for policy & planning. *Journal of Environmental Planning Management*, 50, 2, 211–231.

Pretty, J., Peacock, J., Sellens, M., and Griffin, M. (2005). The mental and physical health outcomes of green exercise. *International Journal of Environmental Health Research*, 15, 5, 319–337.

Primack, Dan. (2015, October 31). The Theranos mess: A timeline. *Fortune*. Accessed at: http://fortune.com/2015/10/31/theranos-timeline/

Prochaska, J. O., Butterworth, S., Redding, C. A., Burden, V., Perrin, N., Leo, M., et al. (2008). Initial efficacy of MI, TTM tailoring and HRI's with multiple behaviors for employee health problems. *Preventive Medicine*, 46, 226–231.

Rabin, M. (1998). Psychology and economics. *Journal of Economic Literature*, 36, 1, 11–46.

Rada, P., Mark, G. P., and Hoebel, B. G. (1998). Galanin in the hypothalamus raises dopamine and lowers acetylcholine release in the nucleus accumbens: A possible mechanism for hypothalamic initiating of feeding behaviour. *Brain Research*, 798, 1–6.

Raymond, N. (2017, February 16). U.S. takes pastor, software developer to trial over bitcoin exchange. *Reuters*. Accessed at: https://www.reuters.com/article/us-cyber-jpmorgan-idUSKBN15U2X1

Rennison, J., and Foley, S. (2015, December 15). Junk bond ETFs hit record trading levels. *Financial Times*. Accessed at: https://www.ft.com/content/68bc8dcc-a2d8-11e5-8d70-42b68cfae6e4

Richards, B. J. (2013, June 10). Acetyl-L-Carnitine delivers fast anti-depressant benefits. *Wellness Resources*. Accessed at: www.wellnessresources.com/health/articles/acetyl-l-carnitine_delivers_fast_anti-depressant_benefits/

Richerson, P. J., Boyd, R., and Henrich, J. (2003). The cultural evolution of human cooperation. In P. Hammerstein (Ed.), *The Genetic and Cultural Evolution of Cooperation* (pp. 357–388). Cambridge, MA: MIT Press.

Robbins, L. (1938). Live and dead issues in the methodology of economics. *Economics*, 5, 342–352.

Robotti, C., and Krivelyova, A. (2003, October). *Playing the field: Geomagnetic storms and the stock market*. Working Paper No. 2003-l5b. Federal Reserve Bank of Atlanta.

Rogers, G., Joyce, P., Mulder, R., Sellman, D., Miler, A., et al. (2004). Association of a duplicated repeated polymorphism in the 5'-untransalted region of the DRD4 gene with novelty seeking. *American Journal of Medical Genetics*, 126B, 95–98.

Roll, R. (1986). The hubris hypothesis of corporate takeovers. *Journal of Business*, 59, 197–216.

Rosen, L. (2015, August 13). Relax, turn off your phone, and go to sleep. *Harvard Business Review*. Accessed at: https://hbr.org/2015/08/research-shows-how-anxiety-and-technology-are-affecting-our-sleep

Rouz, Kristian. (2017, January 12). Overpriced: Trump wipes $24.6 bln off drug and biotech stocks in 20 minutes. *Sputnik International*. https://sputniknews.com/business/201701121049529521-trump-drug-biotech-stocks/

Rubinstein, N. J. (1997), The psychological value of open space. In L. W. Hamilton (Ed.), *The Benefits of Open Space*. Morristown, NJ: The Great Swamp Watershed Association.

Ruhayel, Y., Malm, G., Haugen, T. B., Henrichsen, T., Bjorsvik, C., Grotmol, T., et al. (2007). Seasonal variation in serum concentrations of reproductive hormones and urinary excretion of 6-sulfatoxymelatonin in men living north and south of the Arctic Circle: A longitudinal study. *Clinical Endocrinology* (Oxf), 67, 85–92.

Rumsfeld, D. H. (2002, February 12). *Transcript of Department of Defense News Briefing. Presenter: Secretary of Defense Donald H. Rumsfeld*. US Department of Defense. Accessed at: http://archive.defense.gov/Transcripts/Transcript.aspx?TranscriptID=2636

Salmon, P. (2001). Effects of physical exercise on anxiety, depression, and sensitivity to stress: A unifying theory. *Clinical Psychology Review*, 21, 1, 33–61.

Sandholm, D. (2013, June 27). Blankfein: Market over-reacted to the Fed. *CNBC*. Accessed at: https://www.cnbc.com/id/100849134

Sapra, S., Beavin, L., and Zak, P. (2012). A combination of dopamine genes predicts success by professional wall street traders. *PLos ONE*, 7, 1–7.

Sapra, S. G., and Zak, P. J. (2008). Neurofinance: Bridging psychology, neurology, and investor behavior. Accessed at SSRN: https://ssrn.com/abstract=1323051

Sapra, S. G., and Zak, P. J. (2010). Eight lessons from neuroeconomics for money managers, CFA Institute Research Publications. *Behavioral Finance and Investment Management*, 2, 63–76.

Sartori, S. B., Whittle, N., Hetzenauer, A., and Singewald, N. (2012). Magnesium deficiency induces anxiety and HPA axis dysregulation: Modulation by therapeutic drug treatment. *Neuropharmacology*, 62, 1, 304–312.

Sartre, J.-P. (1943). *Being and Nothingness: A phenomenological essay on ontology*. New York: Philosophical Library.

Saxe, R., and Haushofer, J. (2008). For love or money: A common neural currency for social and monetary reward. *Neuron*, 58, 164–165.

Schjoedt, U., Stodkilde-Jorgensen, H., Geerts, A., Lund, T., and Roepstorff, A. (2011). The power of charisma – perceived charisma inhibits the frontal executive network of believers in intercessory prayer. *SCAN*, 6, 119–127.

Shleifer, A. (2012). Psychologists at the gate: A review of Daniel Kahneman's thinking, fast and slow. *Journal of Economic Literature*, 50, 1–12.

Schrand, C. M., and Zechman, S. L. C. (2012). Executive overconfidence and the slippery slope to financial misreporting. *Journal of Accounting and Economics*, 53, 311–329.

Schreiber, K. (2012). Can we become addicted to stress? *Time*. Accessed at: http://healthland.time.com/2012/09/06/can-we-become-addicted-to-stress/

Schwartz, N., and Bless, H. (1991). Happy and mindless, but sad and smart? The impact of affective states on analytic reasoning. In J. Forgas (Ed.), *Emotion and Social Judgments* (pp. 55–71). Oxford: Pergamon.

Scorsese, M. (Dir.) (2013). *The Wolf of Wall Street*. Red Granite Pictures.

Scully, D., Kremer, J., Meade, M. M., Graham, R., and Dudgeon, K. (1998). Physical exercise and psychological wellbeing: A critical review. *British Journal of Sports Medicine*, 32, 111–120.

SEC. (2016, November 17). *Press Release 2016-241: JPMorgan Chase Paying $264 Million to Settle FCPA Charges*. US Securities and Exchange Commission. Accessed at: https://www.sec.gov/news/pressrelease/2016-241.html

Sent, M. (2004). Behavioral economics: How psychology made its (limited) way back into economics. *History of Political Economy*, 36, 4, 735–760.

Shariff, M. Z., Al-Khasawneh, J., and Al-Mutawa, M. (2012). Risk and reward: A neurofinance perspective. *International Review of Business Research Papers*, 8, 6, 126–133.

Shermer, M. (2006, July 1). The political brain. *Scientific American*. Accessed at: www.scientificamerican.com/article/the-political-brain/

Shiller, R. J. (2003, Winter). From efficient markets theory to behavioral finance. *The Journal of Economic Perspectives*, 17, 1, 83–104.

Shilling, A. (2016, November 22). Record flows to financial sector funds. *Financial Planning*. Accessed at: https://www.financial-planning.com/slideshow/record-flows-to-financial-sector-funds

Shiv, B., and Fodorikhin, A. (1999, December). Heart and mind in conflict: The interplay of affect and cognition in consumer decision making. *Journal of Consumer Research*, 26, 3, 278–292.

Sinclair, E. (2013). *Volatility Trading*. John Wiley & Sons.

Sinha, R. (2008). Chronic stress, drug use, and vulnerability to addiction. *Annals of the New York Academy of Sciences*, 1141, 105–130. Accessed at: www.ncbi.nlm.nih.gov/pmc/articles/PMC2732004/#R28

Smith, A., Lohrenz, T., King, J., Read Montague, P., and Camerer, C. F. (2014, July 22). Irrational exuberance and natural crash warning signals during endogenous experimental market bubbles. *PNAS*, 111, 29, 10503–10508.

Springsteen, B. (1975). Born to run. [Audio recording].

Stadler, C., and Dyer, D. (2013, March 19). Why good leaders don't need charisma. *MIT Sloan Review Magazine*. Accessed at: http://sloanreview.mit.edu/article/why-good-leaders-dont-need-charisma/

Stallen, M., De Dreu, C. K., Shalvi, S., Smidts, A., and Sanfey, A. G. (2012, March 26). The herding hormone: Oxytocin stimulates in-group conformity. *Psychological Science*, 23, 11, 1288–1292.

Stein, C. (2017, January 11). Trump effect triples ETF inflows even before he takes office. *Bloomberg News*.

Steinberg, L. (2010). A dual-systems model of adolescent risk-taking. *Developmental Psychobiology*, 52, 216–224.

Stel, M., and Vonk, R. (2010). Mimicry in social interaction: Benefits for mimickers, mimickees, and their interaction. *British Journal of Psychology*, 101, 311–323.

Stenstrom, E., and Saad, G. (2011). Testosterone, financial risk-taking, and pathological gambling. *Journal of Neuroscience, Psychology, and Economics*, 4, 4, 254–266.

Sterling, P., and Eyer, J. (1988). Allostasis: A new paradigm to explain arousal pathology. In S. Fisher and J. Reason (Eds.), *Handbook of Life Stress, Cognition, and Health* (pp. 629–649). Chichester, UK: John Wiley & Sons.

Stone, O. (Dir.) (1987). *Wall Street*. Twentieth Century Fox.

Stone, O. (Dir.) (2010). *Wall Street: Money Never Sleeps*. Twentieth Century Fox.

Sundby, A. (2010, January 13). Bank execs offer head scratching answers. *CBS MoneyWatch*. Accessed at: https://www.cbsnews.com/news/bank-execs-offer-head-scratching-answers/

Svartberg, J., Jorde, R., Sundsfjord, J., Bonaa, K. H., and Barett-Connor, E. (2003). Seasonal variation of testosterone and waist-to-hip ratio in men: the tromso study. *Journal of Clinical Endocrinology and Metabolism*, 88, 3099–3104.

Tamminen, J., Lambon Ralph, M. A., and Lewis, P. A. (2013). The role of sleep spindles and slow-wave activity in integrating new information in semantic memory. *The Journal of Neuroscience*, 33, 39, 15376–15381.

Tannenbaum, P. H., and Zillmann, D. (1975). Emotional arousal in the facilitation of aggression through communication. In L. Berkowitz (Ed.), *Advances in Experimental Social Psychology* (Vol. 8, pp. 149–192). New York: Academic.

Taylor, S. E., Klein, L. C., Lewis, B. P. Gruenewald, T. L., Gurung, R.A.R., and Updegraff, J.A. (2000). Biobehavioral responses to stress in females: Tend-and-befriend, not fight-or-flight. *Psychological Review*, 107, 3, 411–429.

Tennessen, C. H., and Cimprich, B. (1995). Views to nature: Effects on attention. *Journal of Environmental Psychology*, 15, 77–85.

Terburg, D., Hooiveld, N., Aarts, H., Kenemans, J. L., and van Honk, J. (2011). Eye tracking unconscious face-to-face confrontations: Dominance motives prolong gaze to masked angry faces. *Psychological Science*, 22, 314–319.

Thagard, P. (2003). Conceptual change. In L. Nadel (Ed.), *Encyclopedia of Cognitive Science*. London: Nature Publishing Group.

Thaler, R., (1991). *Quasi-rational Economics*. New York: Russell Sage Foundation.

Thayer, R. E. (1987). Problem perception, optimism, and related states as a function of time of day (diurnal rhythm) and moderate exercise: Two arousal systems in interaction. *Motivation and Emotion*, 11, 19–36.

Thielman, S. (2016, December 12). Trump's tweet about Lockheed-Martin cuts $4bn in value as share prices fall. *Guardian*. Accessible at: https://www.theguardian.com/business/2016/dec/12/lockheed-martin-share-prices-donald-trump-tweet

Thirthalli, J., Naveen, G., Rao, M., Varambally, S., Christopher, R., and Gangadhar, B. (2013). Cortisol and antidepressant effects of yoga. *Indian Journal of Psychiatry*, 55, 7, 405.

Thompson, G. F. (2014). *Globalization Revisited*. New York: Routledge.

Tierney, J (August 17, 2011). 'Do you suffer from decision fatigue?' The New York Times online. Accessed at: http://www.nytimes.com/2011/08/21/magazine/do-you-suffer-from-decision-fatigue.html

Tilbrook, A. J., Turner, A. I., and Clarke, I. J. (2000). Effects of stress on reproduction in non-rodent mammals: The role of glucocorticoids and sex differences. *Review of Reproduction*, 5, 105–113.

Tversky, A., and Kahneman, D. (1974). Judgment under uncertainty: Heuristics and biases. *Science*, 185, 1124–1131.

Ulrich, R. S. (1979). Visual landscapes and psychological wellbeing. *Landscape Research*, 4, 17–23.

Ulrich, R. S. (1981). Natural versus urban scenes: Some psychophysiological effects. *Journal of Environment and Behaviour*, 13, 5, 523–556.

Ulrich, R. S. (1984). Views through a window may influence recovery from surgery. *Science*, 224, 420–421.

Ulrich, R. S. (2002, May 14). *The therapeutic role of green space*. Paper presented at the Greenspace and Healthy Living National Conference, Manchester.

Ulrich, R. S., and Parsons, R. (1992). Influences of passive experiences with plants on individual well-being and health. In D. Relf (Ed.), *The Role of Horticulture in Human Well-Being and Social Development* (pp. 93–105). Portland, OR: Timber Press.

Ulrich, R. S., Simons, R. F., Losito, B. D., Fiorito, E., Miles, M. A., and Zelson, M. (1991). Stress recovery during exposure to natural and urban environments. *Journal of Environmental Psychology*, 16, 3–11.

University of Notre Dame and Labaton Sucharow LLP. (2015, May). *The street, the bull, and the crisis: A survey of the US & UK financial services industry*. Accessed at: https://www.secwhistlebloweradvocate.com/pdf/Labaton-2015-Survey-report_12.pdf

Urschel, J. C., Hu, X., Xu, J., and Zikatanov, L. T. (2014). A Cascadic Multigrid Algorithm for Computing the Fiedler Vector of Graph Laplacians. Cornell University Library. Accessed at: https://arxiv.org/abs/1412.0565

van Honk, J. (1999). Correlations among salivary testosterone, mood and selective attention to threat in humans. *Hormonal Behavior*, 36, 17–24.

Van Honk, J., Schuttera, D. J., Bosa, P. A., Kruijtc, A., Lentjesd, E. G., amd Baron-Cohen, S. (2011). Testosterone administration impairs cognitive empathy in women depending on second-to-fourth digit ratio. *PNAS*, 108, 8, 3448–3452.

Veblen, T. (1898). Why is economics not an evolutionary science? *Quarterly Journal of Economics*, 12, 4, 373–397. Accessed at: http://elegant-technology.com/resource/ECO_SCI.PDF

Veldkamp, L. L. (2005). *Media Frenzies in Markets for Financial Information*. New York University Stern School of Business. Accessed at: http://people.stern.nyu.edu/lveldkam/pdfs/infomkt.pdf

Venkatraman, V., Huettel, S. A., Chuah, L. Y. M., Payne, J. W., and Chee, M. W. L. (2011). Sleep deprivation biases the neural mechanisms underlying economic preferences. *Journal of Neuroscience*, 31, 10, 3712.

Vlastelica, R. (2017, January 10). Here's how much ETFs are dominating on the trading floor. *MarketWatch*. Accessed at: https://www.marketwatch.com/story/heres-how-much-etfs-are-dominating-on-the-trading-floor-2017-01-10

Voracek, M., and Tran, U. (2007). Dietary tryptophan intake and suicide rate in industrialized nations. *Journal of Affective Disorders*, 98, 259–62.

Waggoner, J. (2016, December 9). Who needs ETFs? Nobody, study says. *Investment News*. Accessed at: http://www.investmentnews.com/article/20161209/free/161209918/who-needs-etfs-nobody-study-says

Wallace, D. L., Vialou, V., Rios, L., Carle-Florence, T. L., Chakravarty, S., Kumar, A., Graham, D. L., Green, T. A., Kirk, A., Iñiguez, S. D., Perrotti, L. I., Barrot, M., DiLeone, R. J., Nestler, E. J., and Bolaños-Guzmán, C. A. (2008). The influence of δfosb in the nucleus accumbens on natural reward-related behavior. The Journal of Neuroscience: The Official Journal of the Society for Neuroscience, 28, 41, 10272–10277.

Warren Buffet Way, The. (n.d.) *Wiley Online*. Accessed at: https://www.wiley.com/ WileyCDA/Section/id-817935.html

Washington, George. (1796, September 19). Farewell address. *American Daily Advertiser*. Accessed at: https://www.ourdocuments.gov/doc.php?flash=true &doc=15

Watts, J. M. (2015, October 21). Singapore court finds pastor guilty of $35 million fraud. *Wall Street Journal*. Accessed at: https://www.wsj.com/articles/ singapore-court-finds-megachurch-pastor-guilty-of-embezzling-more-than-35-million-1445412217

Weber, B., Rangel, A., Wibral, M., and Falk, A. (2009, March 31). The medial prefrontal cortex exhibits money illusion. *PNAS*, 106, 13, 5025–5028.

Westen, D., Blagov, P. S., Harenski, K., Kilts, C., and Hamann, S. (2006). Neural bases of motivated reasoning: An FMRI study of emotional constraints on partisan political judgment in the 2004 US presidential election. *Journal of Cognitive Neuroscience*, 18, 11, 1947–1958.

White, R., and Heerwagen, J. (1998). Nature and mental health. In A. Lundberg (Ed.), *The Environment and Mental Health*. Mahwah, NJ: Earlbaum.

Wieczner, J. (2014, February 17). 'Is there a suicide contagion on Wall Street?' *Fortune Magazine Online*. Accessed at: http://fortune.com/2014/02/27/ is-there-a-suicide-contagion-on-wall-street/

Wigglesworth, Robin. (2017, January 24). ETFs are eating the stock market. *Financial Times*. Accessed at: www.ft.com/content/6dabad28-e19c-11e6-9645-c9357a75844a

Winters, S. (2013, April 17). Rogue traders. *CIMA Financial Management Magazine*. Accessed at: www.fm-magazine.com/feature/depth/rogue-traders

Wong, E. M., Ormiston, M. E., and Haselhuhn, M. P. (2011). A face only an investor could love: CEOs' facial structure predicts their firms' financial performance. *Psychological Science*, 22, 1478–1483.

Xenophon. (1994). *Memorabilia*. Trans. Amy L. Bonnette. Introduction by Christopher Bruell. Ithaca: Cornell University Press.

Yarrow, J. F., White, L. J., McCoy, S. C., and Borst, S. E. (2010, July 26). Training augments resistance exercise induced elevation of circulating Brain Derived Neurotrophic Factor (BDNF). *Neuroscience Letters*, 479, 2, 161–165.

Young, S. N. (2007). How to increase serotonin in the human brain without drugs. *Journal of Psychiatry & Neuroscience: JPN*, 32, 6, 394–399.

Zak, J. (2004). Neuroeconomics. *Philosophic Transactions of the Royal Society of London*, 359, 1737–1748.

Zak, P. J., Kurzban, R., Ahmadi, S., Swerdloff, R. S., Park, J., Efremidze, L., et al. (2009, December). Testosterone administration decreases generosity in the ultimatum game. *PLoS ONE*, 4, 12, 1–7.

Zakharov, I. G., and Tyrnov, O. F. (2001). The effect of solar activity on ill and healthy people under conditions of nervous and emotional stresses. *Advances in Space Research*, 28, 4, 685–690.

Zehndorfer, E. (2015). *Charismatic Leadership: The Role of Charisma in the Global Financial Crisis*. London: Routledge.

Zillmann, D. (1998). The psychology of the appeal of portrayals of violence. In J. Goldstein (Ed.), *Why We Watch: The Attractions of Violent Entertainment* (pp. 179–211). New York: Oxford University Press.

Zillmann, D. (2006). Dramaturgy for emotions from fictional narration. In J. Bryant & P. Vorderer (Eds.), *Psychology of Entertainment* (pp. 215–238). Mahwah, NJ: Erlbaum.

Zink, C. F., Pagnoni, G., Martin-Skurksi, M. E., Chappelow, J. C., and Berns, G. S. (2004). Human striatal responses to monetary reward depend on saliency. *Neuron*, 42, 509–517.

Zuckerman, M. (1994). *Behavioral Expressions and Biosocial Bases of Sensation Seeking*. Cambridge, MA: Cambridge University Press.

Zweig, J. (2007). *Your Money and Your Brain*. New York: Simon & Schuster.

Index